T0271171

Monetary Policy and Inflation

Recent years have seen a return to high inflation that has sparked debate about the causal role of monetary policy in significant price increases, especially in the context of the quantity theory of money. This book builds upon a long-accepted tradition of quantity theory of money in explaining long-run inflation levels.

It elucidates how and why – despite its important limitations – the theory can be applied throughout history, including the 2022 spikes in inflation. It also demonstrates how and why the quantity theory, with some internally good reasons, is not part of the modern monetary policy framework. The book argues that firstly, the issue of non-operationability of the money supply is a policy problem, but not a causality problem. Secondly, while some models can work without money, and while a simple deterministic relationship between money base and aggregates may not exist, the author shows that there is still room for quantity theory to be true. Thirdly, perhaps most importantly, as the book shows, the apparent lack of a relationship between the inflation index and money supply with single-digit inflation is a statistical artifact resulting from confounding factors. To conclude, although the quantity theory of money has not been employed in recent Central bank policy, it still holds up surprisingly well in explaining real-world phenomena, including the current record inflation levels.

The practical significance of this book is to illustrate to researchers and scholars how classical macroeconomic thinking can explain key monetary factors that lead to inflation, but also at the same time show that it is fully compatible with modern macroeconomics and is not just a thing of the past.

Mateusz Machaj is a Researcher at the University of New York in Prague and an Associate Professor at the Institute of Economic Sciences, University of Wroclaw, Poland.

Routledge Focus on Economics and Finance

The fields of economics are constantly expanding and evolving. This growth presents challenges for readers trying to keep up with the latest important insights. Routledge Focus on Economics and Finance presents short books on the latest big topics, linking in with the most cutting-edge economics research.

Individually, each title in the series provides coverage of a key academic topic, whilst collectively the series forms a comprehensive collection across the whole spectrum of economics.

Markets vs Public Health Systems
Perspectives from the Austrian School of Economics
Łukasz Jasiński

Public Policy and the Impact of COVID-19 in Europe
Economic, Political and Social Dimensions
Magdalena Tomala, Maryana Prokop and Aleksandra Kordonska

Economic Innovations
Creating New Instruments to Improve Economic Life
Beth Webster and Bill Scales

Well-being and Growth in Advanced Economies
The Need to Prioritise Human Development
Maurizio Pugno

The Economics of ObamaCare
Łukasz Jasiński

Monetary Policy and Inflation
Quantity Theory of Money
Mateusz Machaj

For more information about this series, please visit: www.routledge.com/
Routledge-Focus-on-Economics-and-Finance/book-series/RFEF

Monetary Policy and Inflation
Quantity Theory of Money

Mateusz Machaj

Routledge
Taylor & Francis Group

LONDON AND NEW YORK

First published 2024
by Routledge
4 Park Square, Milton Park, Abingdon, Oxon OX14 4RN

and by Routledge
605 Third Avenue, New York, NY 10158

Routledge is an imprint of the Taylor & Francis Group, an informa business

© 2024 Mateusz Machaj

British Library Cataloguing-in-Publication Data
A catalogue record for this book is available from the British Library

Library of Congress Cataloguing-in-Publication Data
Names: Machaj, Mateusz, author.
Title: Monetary policy and inflation : quantity theory of money / Mateusz Machaj.
Description: Abingdon, Oxon ; New York, NY : Routledge, 2024. | Series: Routledge focus on economics and finance | Includes bibliographical references and index.
Identifiers: LCCN 2023036087 (print) | LCCN 2023036088 (ebook) | ISBN 9781032557991 (hardback) | ISBN 9781032558509 (paperback) | ISBN 9781003432562 (ebook)
Subjects: LCSH: Monetary policy. | Inflation (Finance)
Classification: LCC HG230.3 .M335 2023 (print) | LCC HG230.3 (ebook) | DDC 332.4/6--dc23/eng/20230830
LC record available at https://lccn.loc.gov/2023036087
LC ebook record available at https://lccn.loc.gov/2023036088

ISBN: 978-1-032-55799-1 (hbk)
ISBN: 978-1-032-55850-9 (pbk)
ISBN: 978-1-003-43256-2 (ebk)

DOI: 10.4324/9781003432562

Typeset in Times New Roman
by MPS Limited, Dehradun

To my lovely wife, Paulina.

Contents

List of figures   *viii*
Acknowledgments   *x*

1   BIS report: Welcome to 2023, inflation depends
    on money supply   1

2   Formalized quantity theory of money and Milton
    Friedman's monetary program   7

3   The most important studies in the quantity theory
    of money research in the last 40 years   13

4   Conventional monetary policy and the rationale
    for the absence of money supply in its rules   25

5   Active monetary policy after 2008 and the
    inadequacy of the money multiplier model   34

6   Active monetary policy during the 2020 pandemic   46

7   Conclusions   52

Literature   *55*
Index   *61*

Figures

1.1 Money supply and inflation rates for the period 2020–2022 (Panel A) and money supply and the size of the absolute error in the inflation projection for 2021–2022.   3

2.1 Velocity of money for the aggregate M1. An apparent break in the earlier trend.   11

3.1 Probably the most important macroeconomic graph of the second part of the 20th century. Relationship between long-run monetary growth and levels of inflation between 1960 and 1990. Observations for 110 countries. Data based on the International Monetary Fund from McCandless and Weber (1995).   14

3.2 Adjusted money supply growth that accounts for changes in real output and money demand. The top graph shows a sample of countries with lower inflation from 1970 to 2005. The bottom graph shows the same sample of countries until the adoption of a direct inflation targeting strategy.   18

3.3 Adjusted money supply growth by real output and money demand vs. inflation levels in countries following a direct inflation targeting strategy.   19

5.1 Monetary base in the United States (2001–2010).   38

5.2 Money aggregate M2 in the United States (2001–2010).   40

6.1 Percent growth of monetary base in the United States, monthly percent change compared to year earlier 2000–2023.   48

6.2 Percent growth of money supply M2 in the United States, monthly percent change compared to year earlier 2000–2023.   49

Acknowledgments

I would like to thank Arkadiusz Sieroń and Alicja Sielska for their comments and suggestions on the early version of the draft. I am also grateful to Krzysztof Turowski and Przemysław Rapka for their insight. Special thanks are to Krzysztof Zuber, with whom I had many discussions on monetary issues.

1   BIS report

Welcome to 2023, inflation depends on money supply

In January 2023, a short study appeared in the Bank for International Settlements newsletter with a telling question in its title: *Does money growth help explain the recent inflation surge?* (Borio et al. 2023). While the place of publication does not directly imply institutional endorsement of a particular point of view, it sufficiently lends it prestige. Especially since the authors are none other than the money research experts: Claudio Borio, Boris Hoffmann, and Egon Zakrajšek; all of them being monetary economists who have worked directly for organizations such as the European Central Bank, the Bundesbank, and the Federal Reserve System. The BIS itself is probably the most important organization influential in suggesting directions for the development of banking regulation.

What conclusions do the authors reach? Firstly, the strong dependence of inflation on the rate of growth of the money supply, known from economic history, depends on the inflationary "situation." Where inflation is high, there is an almost one-to-one relationship with the money supply. A higher rate of growth of money aggregates co-occurs with higher inflation. Where inflation is low, such a relationship is virtually nonexistent. As we will see below, this is far from a groundbreaking conclusion, for it is known from previous key publications, including one systematic review that was cited in Robert Lucas's famous Nobel lecture. In view of this, we have a certain economic "law," or if one prefers an economic "regularity," which occurs in two different instances, two different dynamics, depending on the baseline parameter.

Secondly, such a relationship between inflation and the rate of growth in the money supply can also manifest itself in the period of transition from low inflation to high inflation, a period characteristic of the post-Covid years. Significant jumps in the money supply preceded significant jumps in inflation rates occurring after some time, which is particularly evident in countries where growth rates additionally stood out. In principle, it can be said that despite very extensive and meticulous

DOI: 10.4324/9781003432562-1

research on the relationship between money and inflation, a more systematic description of the dynamic transition from one inflationary state
to another is lacking. At high inflation the relationship with the money
supply is evident. At low inflation, such a relationship is not seen. Thus,
we have two different macroeconomic models that are reflected in the
real data (Borio et al. 2023a). An economy of type Y, where there is high
inflation and a strong correlation of money with prices, and an economy
of type X, where there is low inflation and no correlation of money with
prices at all. But after all, these two different economic states, "high
inflation" and "low inflation," are not perfectly dichotomous. There is a
spectrum of lower and higher inflation between economies X and Y. So
there must be some kind of dynamic relationship between these states.
As we move into higher inflationary states, from economy X to economy
Y, the impact or occurrence of significant increments in the money
supply, which could be linked to inflation, should simultaneously appear
in a noticeable dynamic manner. All indications are that the period from
2020 to 2023 is precisely the period of such manifestation.

These two monetary facts, along with the emphasis on the role of
transients, become the rationale for the third conclusion: monitoring
increments in the money supply could improve the quality of inflation
forecasts made for the post-pandemic period (and future similar events).
As a result, it can be said that the informational value of money supply
indicators definitely increased during the pandemic period. Unfortunately,
before that they were evidently depreciated due to the belief that developed
economies were permanently in a state of low inflation (economy type X),
in which the relationship of money supply to prices is simply not empiri-
cally apparent. Meanwhile, if only central banks had taken monetary
aggregates more into account in their decisions, higher inflation could
have been predicted – and, as a natural consequence, could have been at
least partially prevented (or, in fact, not caused) by an unusually loosened
monetary policy. This is clearly reflected in two charts included in the
publication (Figure 1.1).

The relationship is indeed significant, as any difference in the excess
growth of the money supply in 2020 translated into an inflation forecasting error of 0.15 percentage points in 2021–2022.

The authors of the study stipulate that they do not undertake to
resolve to what extent the relationship between inflation and money
supply is causal, that is, whether, for example, there is reverse causality,
or a partially complex relationship involving some feedback loops. It is
also possible that there are influences of other variables that determine to
some extent both simultaneously. Whatever answer is given to this
question, it does not change the fact that the correlation has been perceived, and that it is possible to anticipate the appearance of higher
inflation in the future and may be sufficient to catch sharper increases in

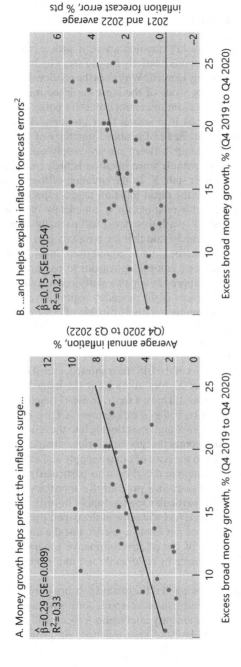

Figure 1.1 Money supply and inflation rates for the period 2020–2022 (Panel A) and money supply and the size of the absolute error in the inflation projection for 2021–2022. (Data for selected OECD countries from Borio et al. 2023.)

monetary aggregates. Even if one questions the direct causality between these quantities, the money supply is an effective anticipatory marker in this case.

In light of such facts, a key question arises: if such a relationship of money to inflation exists and is relatively easy to see, why have monetary aggregates remained largely ignored? Why does the relationship, called the quantity theory of money – one of the most hardened macroeconomic theorems – remain so irrelevant to current monetary policy discourse?

The purpose of this book is to answer these questions. In the briefest of terms, it is partly contained in the above summary of the empirical relationship: the relationship between money supply and inflation is evident and almost indisputable when inflation is high enough, that is, when the economy reflects state Y. In the situation of low inflation, an X-type economy, close to the direct inflation target, especially in single digits below 5 percent, this relationship is completely invisible or, as most claim, "non-existent" (with this view I will partially argue). All in all, under the X realm it can be said that the economy is in a situation of a different category of macroeconomic equilibrium, in which monetary policymakers have their own compelling reasons to pay no attention to the money supply. This approach is particularly reinforced by the fact that, on balance, no designers of the monetary regime have been able to show that targeting the money supply is capable of achieving a specific inflation target in the long run. I intend to show that these two aspects neither undermine the quantity theory of money nor its role in forecasting higher inflations.

Moreover, as the authors of the BIS study showed, even if observing the money supply in economy X does nothing for the immediate inflation target, this observation can still have a separate useful function: a marker for the risk of entering a transition state economy XY, an economy precipitating out of equilibrium X and transitioning into the economy of Y, in which higher inflation becomes the new equilibrium situation.

A reserved approach to the issue of money supply and inflation is also evident among macroeconomic theorists, who particularly point to the failure of the so-called Friedman's program for monetary stability. Its purpose was to target a particular money supply in order to achieve a given rate of price inflation. As I will show in the paper, the failure of the Friedman project also does not imply a rejection of the quantity theory of money, but only one of the positive normative programs that was inspired by it. Mistakes made by children do not imply mistakes on the part of their parents.

It is also worth mentioning that the quantity theory of money, mainly through popularized and simplistic interpretations, was used after 2008 to suggest that excessive monetary interventions by central banks would quickly lead to very high levels of price inflation. As I will show in this book, these suggestions were largely based on an outdated model of the money creation multiplier, in which increases in base money simply translate into increases in actual money in the economy (broad aggregates). This story turned out to be far from the truth, and money growths after 2008 were not at all record-breaking, while they pale in comparison with the period from 2020 onward.

In Chapter 2, I will discuss the basic formalization of the quantity theory of money, known as the equation of exchange, and discuss its usefulness for interpreting various aggregate changes with macroeconomic consequences. I will then show how the equation of exchange was used to present Milton Friedman's monetary program for supposed price and macroeconomic stability. I will also point out the sources of his failure, and how this failure does not entail in any way a rejection of the quantity theory of money.

In Chapter 3, I will discuss the most important empirical studies on the quantity theory of money, which not only remain in force, but in fact, while being conducted by authors who combine into a unified picture. Virtually all of them show that the data on the relationship between prices and money are grouped into two separate states, which for the purposes of our analysis we have named X and Y. In addition, I will show that one of the recent and altogether most important papers on quantity theory, Teles et al. (2016), not only makes a good separation between X and Y, but at the same time shows that the X boundary threshold is much lower than previously thought. Y economies start already above inflation as low as five percent, not at significant double-digit inflation as previously noted. Moreover, the merit of this study, in sum, is that it opens the way to show that the dependence of prices on the quantity of money occurs even in X-type economies, even when a state of stable price equilibrium is reached in which the direct inflation target is realized. This dependence is obscured by other data.

In Chapter 4, I discuss conventional monetary policy, which is built around the concept of targeting definite levels of the inflation basket. Specifically, I discuss how the central bank's nominal interest rates have become the main tool for influencing price increases in the economy. From the perspective of targeting a specific level of positive inflation, it is fully rational and justified by the data to use interest rates instead of using monetary aggregates. A controlled interest rate interacts more or less with all real rates in the economy and activates monetary transmission channels. At the same time – and this was similar in the case of Friedman and the recognition of equilibrium economy X – the depreciation of monetary aggregates in conventional policy does not mean that the quantity theory of money does not apply. Again, its apparent absence from short-term central bank's interventions does not mean that it does not make a significant macroeconomic imprint.

Chapter 5 deals with unconventional monetary policy tools that began to be used after the 2008 crisis. The period is also a sensitive one for quantity monetary theory, as these tools are sometimes associated with monetarist interpretations of the Great Depression. The assumption is that the depth of the Great Depression was due to declines in the money supply, and modern tools are supposed to not only prevent this, but even significantly increase increases in the money supply in line with the money creation multiplier. In fact, the period after 2008 saw record increments in the monetary base and, at the same time, the heyday of journalistic scaremongering about imminent upcoming very high inflation in the United States. Although economists who have been seriously involved in monetary policy for years knew that the mechanistic multiplier description of money creation was wrong, many others only began to learn about it after 2008, because that's when it became clear that the exogenous increase in outside money by the central bank does not automatically translate into an increase in inside money by commercial banks. Again, as in previous cases, the failure of a radical increase in base money to induce the same radical increase in broader monetary aggregates, does not mean that the quantity theory of money does not apply. One might even say that the opposite is true. If radical increases in the monetary base caused increases in inflation without an increase in the broad money supply, then something would not be quite right with the quantity theory.

Finally, in Chapter 6, I show that increments in the money supply proper were at record levels in the twenty-first century and had not previously reached such levels after either the 2001 recession or the 2008 recession. I am specifically referring to broad money aggregates, not the monetary base. The monetary base after 2008 has grown even more than in 2020, but this is irrelevant, as I am not defending the automatic multiplier model of money creation. In contrast, the years since 2020 have been characterized by much larger increments in the money supply than what happened in the previous 20 years. Henceforth – considering the past 40 years of monetary research virtually unanimous on the issue – the explanation for the record inflation spike in the post-pandemic period is available at hand.

I close the study with concluding words and suggestions for future research.

2 Formalized quantity theory of money and Milton Friedman's monetary program

The quantity theory of money is sometimes presented in a formalized way by means of the famous equation of exchange, which in one of its three variants is presented as follows: $MV = PQ$, where M is the money supply in circulation (about the controversy over this in a moment), V is the velocity of circulation, and P is the average price level, while Q is real output. The left side of the equation is simply "money spent," and the right side of the equation is "money received." One, of course, must equal the other.

(A more appropriate form of the equation uses the quantity T, or the number of transactions carried out, instead of Q. However, this is not overly interesting or relevant if we want to analyze more applicable economic variables. That is why Q is used to denote real output, e.g. real GDP, although here too, there is some inaccuracy, since money is not only spent on final goods, included in GDP. Money also goes to intermediate production goods, and in no small amounts, hence it would be more accurate to use global gross spending in this equation).

The equation of exchange shows the quantity theory of money in action, as it mathematically translates, for example, that a 10 percent increase in the money supply means a 10 percent increase in the variable M in the economy. For the equation to remain complete, it is necessary in such a situation to adapt any of the remaining three variables: V, P, or Q. One could, for example, decrease V, which would manifest itself, in the accumulation of "out-of-circulation" means of payment (an increase in demand for money on the part of money holders). However, if this increased money supply is not tucked away in cash balances (V does not fall), this means that either the overall price level P must rise, also by 10 percent, or real output would have to rise for some reason. The monetarist side has tended to bet on the former scenario, arguing that nominal variables go up along with the growth of money in circulation.

The equation itself, however, does not guarantee such a course of action, since there are various combinations of possible changes. At this

DOI: 10.4324/9781003432562-2

point, however, it is worth noting that this equation of exchange is essentially a tautology, which (ignoring the inaccuracy related to GDP) must always be true, since money spent will always equal money received. One cannot spend money if no one receives it, there is no other option. Moreover, the de facto equation is not really dynamic, since there is no possibility that, for example, MV will exceed PQ (or vice versa). At any given time, these variables always equalize. Therefore, in a way, it is confusing to say that money is spent in the market and the prices of goods and services are raised in response. These two things must occur simultaneously, since the flow of money is already taking place at the moment when, based on current valuations and prices in the market, the spending decisions of participants in economic exchange are formed (Salerno 2006). A selected hundred monetary units are not simply spent in the market, but are spent at a certain price on selected goods.

Although the exchange equation is tautological in its formula, it can be used to represent a specific positive monetary policy program formulated by Milton Friedman (Friedman 1956, 1960, 1968, 1969). According to Friedman – like many other theorists – the optimal monetary program should aim at achieving price stability, understood as low positive inflation. This goal itself has never really been sufficiently justified, and is most often based on the tacit assumption of downward nominal rigidity coupled with a specific social utility function. Putting these issues aside, we can contrast Friedman's target with other variables in the exchange equation. If P is to remain stable, what can happen to the other variables? Q, or real output, is assumed to follow a stable long-term growth path (to which, among other things, predictable and conservative monetary policy is supposed to contribute). What remains to be decided are changes to the left-hand side variables, i.e. V and M. As for the velocity rate, at the time of Friedman's publication of his monetary history of the United States (a key Nobel achievement), written together with Anna Schwartz, the rate was considered sufficiently stable with some two exceptions (Friedman and Schwartz 1963).

Or at least that is what empirical observations seemed to suggest. To see how the velocity rate behaves, it can be calculated ex post (that is, not before policy decisions) by dividing nominal income (that is, PQ) by the money supply ratio (M). And until the 1960s, it turned out that this rate was in a stable corridor except in cases of hyperinflation and hyperdeflation (see e.g. Cagan 1956). Hyperinflation essentially consists of very high monthly price increases, and its epidemiology clearly indicates that it occurs in an environment of radical increases in the money supply. On the opposite side, hyperdeflation consists of a situation where there is a radical decline in the money supply, which creates strong deflationary pressures in the economy, described by, among others, the main proponent of the equation of exchange, Irving Fisher (Fisher 1933). These two extreme cases are characterized by behavioral adaptation on the part of market actors. People change their demand for money when prices rise significantly as a result of an increase in the money supply (they reduce their demand i.e. increase their spending). In the opposite situation, they also change their demand for money when there is a banking crisis and a decline in the money supply, but in the other direction. Then this demand increases, i.e. the propensity to spend money decreases. Both of these extreme scenarios are in response to extreme changes in the amount of money in circulation. So, at the time of Friedman's most important publications, one could say that the rate of velocity is virtually stable as long as there are no shocking changes in the money supply.

Thus, adding all these observations together allowed to give birth to a positive monetary program: since in general a constant velocity rate and stable positive growth are possible with sufficiently stable and predictable monetary rules, stable prices will be achieved with a stable monetary program, increasing the money supply in circulation at a rate slightly higher than economic growth. If growth is 2–3 percent, the rate of velocity is constant, and prices are expected to grow by 0–2 percent, then the rate of growth of the money supply should reach 3–5 percent per year. Such a figure is a stable rule for long-term growth, under which velocity should not change radically, therefore the price inflation should not be high.

Despite its undoubted attractiveness and econometric simplicity, however, the program had to fail. Not least because no central bank was interested in depriving itself of discretionary policy. Not least because the program did not necessarily imply a stable macroeconomic situation and sustainable growth, as it did not really preclude the accumulation of unstable investment projects. One of the main and at the same time uncontroversial obstacles was purely technical and struck directly at the simplicity of the model: the assumption of a constant velocity of money broke down. This is because it turned out that the rate of velocity since the 1970s has not held as steady as it did in the times analyzed by Friedman and Schwartz.

The failure of a positive monetary program is also sometimes presented in the form of the suggestion that it is not very clear which money supply rate should be chosen for targeting to achieve certain levels of inflation. However, this is not really a separate argument, but a variation of the one about the velocity of circulation. Doubts about the feasibility of choosing the right money supply indicator stem, among other things, from the lack of constancy in the rate of circulation. This is because there is simply no money supply indicator that moves at a similar rate over an extended period of time as nominal income. And, after all, the ratio of nominal income to the chosen monetary aggregate is nothing other than the rate of circulation of money, according to the tautological construction of the equation of exchange. If we were to choose such a monetary aggregate M, at which its ratio to PQ remains constant for a sufficiently long period of time, then we would find an aggregate that could perhaps be targeted.

The vagaries of these parameters, meanwhile, mean that choosing one particular money supply indicator would be unlikely to help a particular inflation target. If one were to choose, for example, a fairly narrow money supply, say M1 (deposits and base money), then banks could shift payment systems to instruments broader than M1 (towards M2). The same goes for following the M2 ratio. Banks could offer alternative instruments, which would mean that monetary demand could be shifted between aggregates, in effect making a positive monetary program not so easy to implement.

This is the reason for the instability of the velocity of money: from financial innovation and the increasing competitiveness of the banking sector. Somewhat paradoxically, Friedman's own promoted market mechanism unleashed natural competitive impediments to his most interventionist program for the banking sector. Nota bene, the Chicago School tradition had already suggested much before him the need for a monetary system in which the money supply in circulation remained under the full control of government agencies (e.g. the central bank). In practice, this would mean a system with 100 percent mandatory deposit coverage by banknotes, coins, and reserves issued by the central bank (with the possible addition of treasury bonds – a solution that would certainly please fiscal policymakers).

Such a system has not been tested anywhere, of course, but it has remained in the realm of intriguing theoretical deliberations, and this has come from a very spectacular group of economists who have played groundbreaking roles in the history of monetary thought (Allais 1987; Fisher 1936; Friedman 1960; Tobin 1985; Merton and Bodie 1993). Although full bureaucratic control of the money supply remained a theoretical pipe dream, deliberations about it reverberated realistically in macroeconomic thinking. The record inflation of the stagflationary period of the 1970s in Western countries added fuel to the fire. It was when a pressure to control the amount of money supply in circulation began to appear in public discourse on monetary policy. At the same time, this was the highest point of monetarism's popularity, from which a natural retreat began, resulting from the changes in the rate of circulation that we have marked. The collapse of the key variable is well reflected in Figure 2.1.

In describing this historical period, Hafer and Wheelock (2001) point out that whether or not we agree that monetarism had its moment in monetary policy, it began to fade after 1980. Monetarism is understood as two interconnected suggestions: that nominal income is the key in

Velocity of Money (M1)
Quarterly Data, 1960 Through 1999

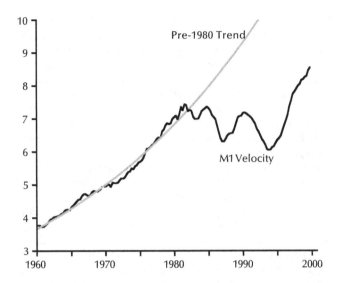

Figure 2.1 Velocity of money for the aggregate M1. An apparent break in the earlier trend (From Hafner and Wheelock 2001.)

macroeconomic fluctuations, and that targeting it with a chosen money supply indicator will achieve the required systemic stability. Due to the aforementioned financial innovations, banks began to offer completely new instruments to reshuffle cash balances, which did not go unnoticed in the velocity of circulation. The stable increments of this parameter seen in the figure began to be unpredictable, and the monetarist-inspired St. Louis models were no longer reliable. The decade of the 1980s was becoming a period in which the greatest proponents of short-term control of the money supply gradually began to give up. In another empirical study, Estrella and Mishkin (1997) proved that, assuming standard "requirements" for monetary policy rules, these rules could not be effectively and operationally based on money supply growth.

The very closure and capitulation in this regard of the monetarist tradition is well illustrated by the words of Milton Friedman himself a few years before his death: "The use of quantity of money as a target has not been a success. I'm not sure I would as of today push it as hard as I once did." (London 2003). Indeed, but this does not simultaneously end the role of quantity of money in circulation.

The quantity theory of money ran through macroeconomic consider-ations preceding the beginnings of the science of economics itself, both with the classics and also long before the founding fathers of the discipline, namely Adam Smith and Richard Cantillon (Locke 1963; Cantillon 1959; Hume, 1777; Cairnes 1873). It was understood as a certain relationship between the amount of money in circulation and price levels, recognizing that in times when the scarcity of money decreases, nominal prices tend to rise. As the science was formalized, it took the form of the famous equa-tion of exchange, in which three combined variables (the demand of money holders, the supply of production and the supply of money) together co-determine final price levels (Bordo 1989). This equation became the field for macroeconomic illustrations of various monetary programs, including the particular one associated with Milton Friedman, as well as his predecessors from the Chicago school.

At the same time, it is crucial in this whole story to recognize that the positive monetary program put forward by Friedman and others is not a quantity theory of money. Suggesting such an overreaching affinity makes two fundamental mistakes. First, the program itself falls within the scope of normative economics and is not a pure economic theory, but a concrete interventionist project. Second, in its essence, it is based on the adoption of specific parameters, relationships and the effects of their interaction. While this is done using tools associated with the broadly understood quantity theory of money, the theory itself does not assume exactly such parameters and norms. Milton Friedman used to say that inflation is always and ev-erywhere a monetary phenomenon. Meanwhile, the quantity theory of money, or the equation of exchange, assumes nothing of such a univer-salist nature, since it takes into account the other two variables besides the money supply in its deliberations. Even if the monetarist program requires the truth of the quantity theory of money, the theory does not require the monetarist program to be true and correct.

In conclusion, the demise of Friedman's monetary program cannot automatically mean the demise of quantity theory, since this program is a normative project built on a combination of quantity theory with some selected empirical assumptions and assumptions about the supposed optimality of a given monetary program. It would therefore be a mistake to throw the baby out with the bathwater. What, then, would a quantity theory of money be after the death of the monetarist program? It would be a thesis that increases in the money supply exert upward pressure on price increases, and this relationship should be all the more apparent as the larger these increases are (on possible meanings of the quantity theory see Sumner 2021). This is what has been established in the major empirical studies presented in the next chapter.

3 The most important studies in the quantity theory of money research in the last 40 years

The quantity theory of money has never really been discarded or permanently forgotten. It plays at least a starter role in understanding the course of macroeconomic processes and appears from time to time in modern empirical studies of major scientific journals. In its core form, it says that there is a long-term relationship between the amount of money in circulation and the final prices of goods and services (and not with real output). Perhaps the strongest empirical argument in its defense was presented in the classic McCandless and Weber (1995) text, which was essentially something like a meta-analysis of the effects of the money supply on the consumer goods price index. This graph was presented by Robert Lucas (1996) in his famous Nobel lecture and is presented in Figure 3.1.

The analysis covered a 30-year period (1960–1990) using a total of 110 different countries as examples. It remains debatable, of course, how exactly to pair the money supply and price index variables together. Whether to look at the relationships in the short or long term, and whether to choose cross-sectional studies, or whether to include lags. Here, the authors decided to focus on a cross-sectional approach because it means freeing themselves from specific policy considerations and the chosen financial architecture. Betting on a pool of more than a hundred countries avoids this problem in part because in such a heterogeneous sample, the distortions of the chosen monetary policy rules become potentially random (although, as we will see below, the problem arises when stratifying countries according to the direct inflation targeting strategy, which leads to splitting countries into two groups: type X economies and type Y economies). We have, of course, other analyses, such as the noteworthy Dewald and Haug (2004) study over as many as 120 years – albeit limited to 11 developed industrialized countries. In this analysis, the authors conclude that the data are consistent with quantity theory. Money supply does not translate into real economic growth, and its main relationship is with nominal output and the final price level.

DOI: 10.4324/9781003432562-3

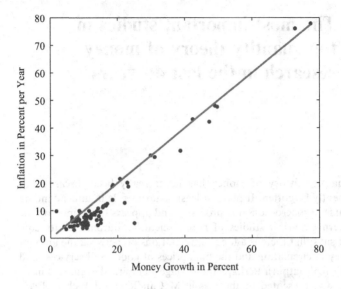

Figure 3.1 Probably the most important macroeconomic graph of the second part of the 20th century. Relationship between long-run monetary growth and levels of inflation between 1960 and 1990. Observations for 110 countries. Data based on the International Monetary Fund from McCandless and Weber (1995) (Redrawn with permission by Teles et al. 2016.)

The correlation itself for a large pool of countries over a long time horizon virtually always comes out striking – rarely in the social sciences do we see such a strong relationship, confirmed in this case by a correlation of 95 percent. An increase in the M2 money supply corresponds closely to an increase in the price index for final goods and services. However, as is the case with such correlations, the matter can get complicated. First of all, a basic principle of aggregate studies dictates that it is always a good idea to do a subgroup analysis and see if the correlation does not occur only with additional characteristics. Something that is strong and true for large groups may look quite different when we make alternative stratifications. Second, it is worth considering the issue of potential feedback or reverse causality between these variables. The money supply grows with price levels, but what is the key driving force here? In his textbook on monetary policy, Walsh (2017, p. 2) makes the argument that theoretically it could be that other factors generate inflation and the central bank "allows" the money supply to adjust.

Starting with the challenge of causality, it is worth bearing in mind that price increases and increases in the money supply are not genetically linked. It may, of course, be the case that certain price movements change the expectations of market actors and lead to adaptation, including when it comes to monetary transmission issues. After all, there is no deterministic prohibition that some economic data cannot change the behavior of market actors, including banks that extend credit (and thus expand the money supply). However, this does not change the fact that price movements do not themselves build the financial architecture or one or another banking system. These are always the result of a certain regulatory design and legal order. If, for example, the monetary system does not allow monetary expansions, then it is not all the same as how final prices will behave – they will not be able to trigger increases in the money supply. What's more, the lack of such opportunities will tend to prevent sustained inflationary spirals. So, responding to Walsh: what if the central bank "does not allow" the money supply to adjust in a short-term upward price shock? Or more extreme, what if the banking system relied on a Fisherian plan to provide access to 100 percent reserves on all deposits? It is difficult to assume then that the money supply would spontaneously follow the earlier price increases. Rather, it would have become a significant brake on such upward trends.

Equally interesting remains the first issue, concerning the study of inflation dependence in subgroups, when a closer look at the research sample allows one to see the basket of X economies and basket of Y economies mentioned in the introduction. For although the meta-analysis looks spectacular for 110 countries at quite a spread of inflation, with more careful decomposition the matter looks quite different. It turns out that the correlation between growth in the money supply and the rising price index for goods and services works great for inflation that enters double-digit levels. Unfortunately, below ten percent the correlation begins to break down, not to say that from a certain point of view simply disappears. That is, the subgroup analysis suggests to us that the quantity theory of money in the "money growth yields a corresponding increase in inflation" version seems to work well only when there are obvious significant increases in the money supply and when inflation is high. However, when inflation is stable, low, and increments in the money supply are not rapid, the correlation does not exist.

De Grauwe and Polan (2005) pinpointed exactly this using an even larger sample of 160 countries over the period 1969–1999. Using International Monetary Fund data, both the M1 and M2 aggregates were checked. Essentially, at the general level of the result, they resemble the study by McCandless and Weber (1995) and other earlier ones (Dwyer and Hafer 1988; Dwyer and Hafer 1999; Vogel 1974). Although the same relationship between money and prices has been established for the aggregate as a whole, it is not perfectly proportional. Its significant impact is evident for Y-type economies, but no longer for X-type economies. This study, on the other hand, classifies not by low inflation per se, but by relatively low money supply growth, specifically 10 percent. For countries that have such long-run average growth in monetary aggregates, the correlation with the final price level is weak. De Grauwe and Polan studied the correlations for different growth thresholds, 10, 20, 30, and so on percent. This confirmed the separation into two types of countries X and Y, but at the same time the separation is gradual. In other words, there is a spectrum between the two ideal types. So, the transition from type X (low inflation, no correlation of money and price) to type Y (high inflation, strong correlation) is gradual, step by step. Quantity theory of money is, of course, also related to the second important macroeconomic conclusion, related to the pro-inflationary nature of money supply growth. Since increments in the money supply translate mainly into nominal price increases in the long run, real economic growth should not depend in the long run on the rate of growth of monetary aggregates. And this observation was established in this study as in others. However, the case of X-type economies, where the equilibrium price-money relationship does not seem to exist, remains a challenge. Another important review reached similar conclusions (Gertler and Hofmann 2018).

Does this mean that the inflationary relationship with the money supply only works at double-digit inflation, and no longer at single-digit inflation? In view of this, are we dealing with the discovery of a kind of multiverse of macroeconomic theories? Or, as Sargent and Surico (2011) suggest, can we say that the basic parameters are changing, de facto undermining the traditional quantity dependence theory?

The answer to this dilemma was provided by one of the most important studies of recent years conducted by Teles et al. (2016). The classical quantity theory of money is formulated in a qualitative way, which, as critics would note, is sometimes difficult to quantify concretely. In fact, the only sensible quantitative approach is the equation of exchange. However, as we know from the equation of exchange, the price level does not depend only on the increment in the money supply. The price index is dependent on the nominal amount of money supply in circulation and two other important variables: real output and the "velocity of money."

$$P = MV/Y$$

Translating this equation into empirical reality is difficult, but some approximation is possible. One can, let's say, more simplistically take real GDP as real output – although as we have already discussed this raises obvious problems related to the fact that money that "circulates" in the economy is not only spent on transactions for final goods (i.e. those included in GDP). An important part of the goods purchased in the market is intermediate production or financial goods. Putting this limitation aside, Teles et al. (2016) made correlations similar to those of McCandless and Weber, pointing out that after a proper output adjustment, the relationship between the quantity of money supply and the price index looks much better.

However, the update does not stop there, for the model also needs to take into account the rate of velocity, which expresses the demand for money. In a classically Fisherian approach, this is of course impossible, since the equation of exchange is tautological, and the rate of circulation is calculated simply by dividing nominal GDP by the chosen money supply index. This procedure makes sense only if we want to check whether a given money supply aggregate is permanently correlated with the nominal size of GDP (in such a way that the ratio of nominal GDP to this aggregate would always be constant, which would imply a constant rate of circulation). It is different, however, when one wants to use non-residually calculated data to make economic predictions. For this purpose, Teles et al. (2016) decided to use the money demand models developed by Miller and Orr (1966), as well as Tobin (1956) and Baumol (1987).

The purpose was to see if the statistical relationship between the quantity of money and price levels could also be reproduced for lower inflation, i.e. X-type economies, as a result of the model adjustment. The data seemed to contradict such a possibility, and placed a cut-off point between economies X and Y at inflation levels as high as 12 percent. Meanwhile, as a result of adjusting the model for the money demand factor and real output, the authors managed to highlight the same relationship as in the original chart – in which case the adjusted increase in money supply translates proportionally into higher levels of inflation. It is shown in Figure 3.2.

The first chart covers the period from the 1970s to 2005. Instead of the conventional year 2005, one can take the adoption as a cut-off point of a direct inflation targeting strategy for the selected country. Then countries that bet on such a strategy are automatically excluded from the graph. As the bottom graph in Figure 3.2 illustrates, the observation becomes even stronger: growth in the money supply adjusted for the rate of circulation and real output correlates very well with inflation growth.

Why exclude countries with a direct inflation targeting strategy from the subgroup analysis? Because (as also shown in the study) in the case of central banks pursuing this strategy, something very peculiar happens: the relationship known from quantity theory cannot be shown even after adjusting for the two key variables we are talking about. Then it simply does not exist, and we enter a pure ideal X-type economy, that is, a low-inflation economy in which the translation of the money supply into prices does not appear. This is shown in Figure 3.3.

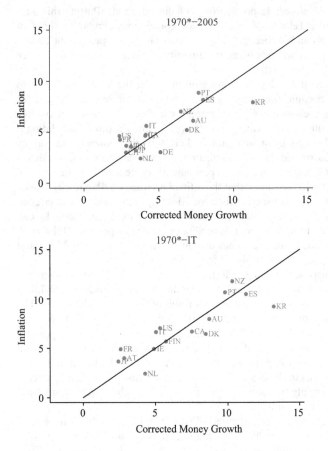

Figure 3.2 Adjusted money supply growth that accounts for changes in real output and money demand. The top graph shows a sample of countries with lower inflation from 1970 to 2005. The bottom graph shows the same sample of countries until the adoption of a direct inflation targeting strategy (From Teles et al. 2016.)

What is special about the direct inflation targeting (DIT) strategy is that many central banks at the turn of the century managed to get on a path of controlled and low inflation, not just single-digit inflation, but inflation below five percent. With the low volatility of low inflation, it is difficult even after adjusting the data to find a translation of the money supply into inflation. Teles et al. (2016) explain the collapse of the relationship of money supply to the price index due to the existence of a successful DIT strategy. The experience of 2020–22 – when, after all, the

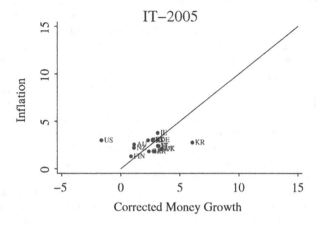

Figure 3.3 Adjusted money supply growth by real output and money demand vs. inflation levels in countries following a direct inflation targeting strategy.

Source: From Teles et al. (2016.)

direct inflation targeting strategy was not abandoned – teaches us that this is not due to the very nature of the DIT, but simply to the fact that inflation was low. And when it becomes high, the correlation is able to return with the same force as demonstrated in the past. However, this article seems to have found the cutoff point between economy X and economy Y at a much lower than double-digit level – around five percent.

Still one can ask the question in terms of the scheme of the equation of exchange – once the variables are taken into account, shouldn't it be the case that the relationship must be apparent one-to-one even at low levels of inflation? Of course it would, but that would be the case assuming that the estimates of both the money supply, the rate of velocity and real output are hit. However, there is a serious risk of errors of a few percent, which can add up to the non-existence of a statistical relationship. Orr's, Tobin's and Baumol's models do not guarantee a perfect account of the velocity of money (especially since financial entities may, at low inflation and DIT, adjust their demand for assets to short-term inflation readings[1]). The same is true of the chosen measure of the money supply or the way real output is measured (which, by the way, does, after all, partially incorporate price increases). Taken together, these imperfections in the data can explain the lack of correlation of the money supply with inflation levels without much trouble when inflation is below 5 percent and when we are talking about the macroeconomic equilibrium of an X-type economy. When, on the other hand, inflation becomes (along with increases in the money supply) high enough, then monetary variables begin to clearly dominate over the others and tip the correlation scales in their favor, becoming fully visible and difficult to question. At the same time, this does not mean that the dependence of prices on money at low inflation does not exist. It can be obscured by other factors.

In summary, therefore, the long-run relationship between money and prices is observable in empirical studies to a wider extent than was thought at the beginning of the twenty-first century, because it also applies to countries with inflation of more than five percent, not just to countries with double-digit inflation. To some extent, the gray and uncertain area remains with X-type economies, i.e. those that pursue a direct inflation targeting strategy (actual low inflation) and achieve a kind of macroeconomic equilibrium with no correlation between the amount of money in circulation and final price levels. However, even in the absence of such correlation, it is not said that actual causality is canceled.

Note

1 De Grauwe and Polan (2005), on the other hand, saw in their analysis that the lack of a relationship between money and prices in X economies is most likely due to an inverse relationship between the rate of growth of the money supply and the velocity, while in Y countries the relationship is positively correlated. This approach could suggest that in equilibrium X there is a kind of overlap between market expectations and the realization of the inflation target directly. That is, of course, until money growth breaks down these expectations.

Appendix to Chapter 3: Epidemiology of hyperinflation

As we saw in Chapter 3, the relationship between the amount of money in circulation and the correspondingly emerging inflation becomes evident in the case of Y-type economies, i.e. economies where inflation exceeds the relevant threshold (between 5 and 12 percent, depending on the research conducted). It becomes all the more unambiguous, of course, in the case of inflation of several hundred percent, or monthly inflation exceeding 50 percent – the conventional threshold at which a country enters a dramatic hyperinflationary path.

Recently, some economists, especially those associated with the Modern Monetary Theory, have begun to suggest that the radical increase in the money supply is not the main cause of hyperinflation. The most common explanation that comes up is that the increase in the money supply (combined with hyperactive fiscal policy) is the result of hyperinflationary tendencies in the economy. Well, it seems that the issue really comes down to how one understands the term "causality" – the real bane not only for the science of economics, but also of many other disciplines, wasting an incredible amount of time on philosophical deliberations about the status of this magical term.

Leaving methodological issues aside, however, the phenomenon of hyperinflation can be treated strictly epidemiologically. Since hyperinflation is the worst disease that money can contract (as it leads to its potential death), there is nothing left to do but to analyze it the same way as other diseases are analyzed: through the prism of the risk factors present in its case with a proper set of causal criteria known from epidemiological studies. The classics, in this case, are the so-called Bradford Hill criteria (started for cigarette smoking and lung cancer), which speak of the necessary following elements (Fedak et al. 2015): 1) Strength of association, 2) Consistency (reproducibility), 3) Specificity, 4) Temporality, 5) Dose-response relationship, 6) Plausibility, 7) Coherence, 8) Experiment, 9) Analogy.

Thus, for example, in cardiology, it is recognized that lipoproteins containing on their surface the so-called alipoprotein B are atherogenic and thus cause cardiovascular disease. Population and clinical evidence accumulated on this issue indicates that the association is: strong, reproducible, specific, temporal, dose-dependent, biologically plausible, coherent with background knowledge, referred to many experiments, referred to analogies. It is also reversible as many intervention studies demonstrated.

How to apply a similar approach to the case of monetary agony? For such an analysis of hyperinflation, two of the best studies will be necessary, which, surprisingly, have been realized only in the last few years. Nota bene it is disappointing that this worst monetary disease, which led not only to economic but also social decay, lived to see systematic reviews only in the twenty-first century. Two publications are involved. One is a compilation of all previous hyperinflations (Hanke and Krus 2012), and the other is the first systematic book on it (Liping 2017). Thanks to them, it becomes clear that the relationship between money supply hypergrowth and hyperinflation is strongly confirmed in epidemiological analyses. This relationship is confirmed by the strength of an association – it already starts with inflation in the 5–12 percent range. The association is reproducible – it occurs in many cases, meticulously documented by Hanke and Krus. This is because it appears in different populations, different cultures, and different political systems. A single hyperinflation study, after all, cannot determine the relationship itself. If, however, we have dozens of them in very different periods, the evidence becomes richer.

The third factor, specificity, is particularly interesting, because in the case of hyperinflation it shows that its causal link is even stronger than in medical science. Heart disease happens at lower levels of alipoprotein B. Lung cancer also happens among non-smokers. So these are ailments that do not have a single exclusive factor indicated in these examples. Meanwhile, hyperinflation provides us with full specificity for mega-increases in the money supply: we simply do not know of any historical case of monetary decay with which there were no radical prior increases in the money supply. It is significant that the listings in the Hanke and Krus table include only two cases of hyperinflation that did not occur in the twentieth century: Zimbabwe in 2007 and France during the revolution. All the other dozens of countries experienced hyperinflation in the twentieth century, and for good reason: because it is the age of political innovation, of pure paper fiat money, allowing unlimited increases in the amount of currency in circulation. Needless to say, France and Zimbabwe are not exceptions to this feature, even though their cases happened in another time. In fact, it can be added here that the Hanke and Krus table omitted the Chinese case a few centuries earlier (although it would be difficult to gather exact numbers in its case). But this case, too, after all, involves paper currency. Thus, one can comfortably conclude that an absolutely necessary risk factor for hyperinflationary disease is monopolistically created and hyperinflated fiat money by the state. Without this factor, hyperinflation has never happened in history. The specificity could hardly be stronger. In this respect, the science of economics – a very rare thing – has managed to surpass the accuracy of biological science.

The fourth factor relates to the temporality of the relationship and is fairly easy to meet with historical data. Eventually, it would be difficult to suggest that price hyperinflation was caused by increases in the money supply that occurred sometime later (although hyperinflationary expectations can, of course, precede later increases – which does not change the fact that they will be broken if increases do not happen). The fifth factor, i.e. dose dependence, also has strong support in the data, for as we have seen, this dependence is already evident for Y economies, i.e. entering double-digit inflation for good. The sixth factor, namely plausibility, is also confirmed. For we have a mechanistic and plausible explanation for the hyperinflationary effect of money supply growth. As the amount of a given monetary aggregate in circulation increases, the nominal incomes of market actors increase. Thus, the marginal value of the monetary unit falls, which then has the effect of reducing the enlarged balances and begins to exert such a change in valuations toward real goods and services. The process ends up with a new arrangement of final prices that are higher than the previous ones. Or to put it more simply, more money circulates, which puts an upward pressure on prices. These increases are not local, as spending bidding occurs in principle in virtually all markets, since almost everyone experiences increases in nominal income sooner or later.

The seventh factor concerns the consistency of a given relationship with the background knowledge of a given discipline. Of course, the monetary background of hyperinflation is as consistent as possible with both macroeconomic and microeconomic knowledge. The theories of money demand and utility are fully compatible (and even require it) with the fact that hyper increments in the quantity of monetary funds will lead to breakthrough increments in the final price level. The eighth factor concerns correlation experiments. The issue of the possibility of experimentation in the social sciences is fundamentally different from how experimentation is understood in the medical sciences. And this is especially true for the issue of experimentation on a nationwide scale, where it is impossible to build a "control group." Nevertheless, to some extent, each individual case of hyperinflation can in fact be treated as an economic experiment on society. And especially with regard to its finale – the timing of the end of hyperinflation, most often by the introduction of a new currency – as a certain symbol to send a signal to market actors that the past will not be repeated. In a way, the reversibility criterion could be a separate Bradford Hill category, but overall it falls under the experimental factor. And so it would be with hyperinflationary economies, which to themselves are an imperfect control group – the moment the government stops printing money, the hyperinflation naturally ends after a while.

The ninth factor regarding analogy is also easy to meet. To hit it, one must find a similar disease where an analogous factor can cause it. Well, practically all other commodities show a similar relationship to money – in a situation where there is a huge increase on the supply side, with it comes a decrease in value. This is the case not only with fiat money, but with gold, rai stones or potatoes and soap.

Hence, applying Bradford Hill's epidemiological criteria, one can conclude that hyperinflation is always and everywhere a hyper-monetary phenomenon. History knows no exception to this rule. Record increases in the money supply have been an absolutely necessary factor for hyper-inflation, without which no case of rapid monetary collapse has been recorded. However, one may ask, in addition to being an absolute factor, is it also an exclusive factor? Here the matter becomes more complicated because social and political systems are characterized by record levels of complexity. Record increments in the money supply must occur. Most often someone (albeit not always) must make a political decision to have the money supply increased in this way. There is absolutely no obstacle to such decisions than being related to other risk factors. In the end, the fact that hyper-increases in the money supply are poison to the money is not surprising and is usually known to political dissidents. The fact that they go for it – or that they risk the occurrence of hyperinflation – means that for some reason they are willing to take that risk. It could be the unavailability of fiscal resources, it could be political decay, it could be desperation, it could even be simple ignorance. A combination of these or other factors comes into play. But high monetary expansion has to happen and other factors do not need to.

The snag is that none of these factors have been worked with Bradford Hill's criteria. None of these factors has been proven to be absolutely necessary and completely sufficient for hyperinflation to occur. Risk factors can be "reduced" in any historical case in an analogous way. Does smoking cause lung cancer? Perversely, and here one can also practice various reductionisms: it is not smoking that causes lung cancer, but stress that leads to smoking. Maybe hard work? Maybe social pressure? Maybe the taste of a cigarette? The point at which reductionism goes too far is when it has failed to deterministically link a given factor to others preceding it. So for the time being, we recognize that smoking causes lung cancer just as we recognize that hyperinflation is caused by too much growth in the money supply. This factor is entirely sufficient for a monetary meltdown to occur and, in principle, must necessarily occur for it to happen.

4 Conventional monetary policy and the rationale for the absence of money supply in its rules

Since the relationship between money supply and inflation is only apparent at high levels (Y economies), it becomes partially understandable why targeting the money supply does not play a role in conventional monetary policy, and is based on a direct inflation targeting strategy, combining many different traditions from the past (see on this Goodfriend and King 1997). We have seen that even when attempting to clean the data by the rate of circulation and real output, the relationship between prices and money fails to be captured to the extent that it is "operationally" beneficial, that is, in the sense that a specific interventionist program could be implemented on it. Steering the money supply to tap into specific levels of increases in the retail price index will probably not work.

However, there is an even stronger and more pragmatic argument for central banks not to focus on the money supply indicator: other operational variables are available (in particular, interest rates) that fit more clearly into the DIT strategy. Many studies in recent decades have indicated that it is easier to realize a chosen level of inflation through interest rate actions, rather than some chosen monetary aggregate that could be consistently adhered to. As a result, the state of monetary policy for the twenty-first century is quite paradoxical: we have a monetary policy without money (McCallum 2001). Hamlet without the ghost (Laidler 2002). This happens altogether even when the central bank rhetorically declares at least a partial commitment to monetary aggregates. A textbook example of this would be the European Central Bank – with its traditional two-pillar strategy, which involved, on the one hand, a price-formation focus and, somewhere in the background, an examination of the long-term relationship between money and prices. In fact, the second part of this strategic statement is a certain relic of the approach from the Bundesbank, which was one of the most important in the formation of the common eurozone. Due to historical experience with very high inflation, German monetary authorities have a greater affinity for focusing directly on monetary brakes. However, this is an

DOI: 10.4324/9781003432562-4

approach from the past that does not impinge too much on the current functioning of the ECB. As a recent analysis has shown, the reference to the monetary aspect is rather pro forma (Gros and Capolongo 2019). Yet the recent rise in inflation may change that.

In the era of forgetting the quantity theory of money, macro models used by central banks very often focus on the monetary transmission mechanism, which is based on the non-neutrality of money, a concept related to the quantity theory in the Walrasian equilibrium framework juxtaposed with frictional reality. If one were to imagine a perfectly adjusting economy in which prices are set continuously and instantaneously, any monetary impulse would have an immediate effect on them without any delay. Output and global demand would reach their "natural" (however that word is understood) levels without any frictions associated with at least nominal rigidities. Many empirical analyses show, of course, that this is never the case, and that monetary policy affects real variables at least in the short term (in the long term, in principle, too, although here much depends on the definition of neutrality and non-neutrality).

The economy does not immediately experience the ideal Fisher effect, which would predict nominal interest rates rising to reach natural real levels as a result of rising inflation. Therefore, traditional central bank actions have significant macroeconomic effects. An example of the traditional New Keynesian description is as follows: a decrease in nominal interest rates also translates into a decrease in real interest rates. This results in an increase in aggregate demand at given nominal volumes. Subsequently, greater supply capacity raises marginal costs and is reflected by this price-generating behavior, increasing inflationary tendencies in the economy in general. In an ideal Walrasian equilibrium situation, such dynamics should not occur at all, and all prices, including the intertemporal price, should adjust perfectly to the new situation without any disturbances in aggregate demand, supply, and other real factors. De facto this would mean monetary superneutrality (Zimmerman 2003, p. 63). Under such conditions, the Fisher effect would always and immediately occur, and the nominal interest rate would always rise with inflation so that the real rate would still be at the same level.

Interest rates have come to the center of monetary policy precisely because of their real consequences and have pushed out monetary aggregates, even if the latter still occupy a readable place in most macroeconomic textbooks. Rate disturbances caused by central banks' policies are being modeled in more and more detail in individual markets. Hence, the aforementioned Fisher effect gap is presented in monetary transmission mechanisms through various channels (Bernanke and Gertler 1995; Brunner and Meltzer 1988; Lown and Morgan 2002; Boivin et al. 2010; Meltzer 1995; Miron et al. 1993). The first four traditional channels are associated with the neoclassical tradition: consumption, investment, international, and the expectations channel.

The consumption channel relies on income and substitution effects for intertemporal allocation. A reduced interest rate affects the prices of owned property, raising its value. The most responsive to this situation generally seem to be younger borrowers who own property on credit. It is in their case to a greater extent that there is a heightened propensity to adjust the size of debt in response to interest rate movements, which affects the elasticity of consumer spending. The heterogeneity of these consumer adaptations can, incidentally, be reconciled with life-cycle theory, and this would explain reasonably well the extent of variation in the subjects' responses (Wong 2019).

The investment channel of transmission, on the other hand, is classically linked to the conventional model. A reduction in interest rates means a reduction in the cost of raising capital (which is a real, not a nominal, effect). Thus, a reduction in interest rates has a short-term effect on spending on capital goods, and thus on overall output and its prices (Brinkmeyer 2015). In essence, this channel can be seen as a user-cost channel. Another element of the investment channel relates to the famous Tobin's q, that is, the market value of a company divided by the cost of reproducing capital (Tobin 1969). In this case, we can speak of the classic asset-price channel, which also falls into the investment chain. In booming times, the market value of companies in the capital market rises relative to the cost of reproducing the assets they hold. Therefore, in times of lower interest rates associated with prosperity, the Tobin factor increases, which further encourages investment in equities (Jeenas and Lagos 2022).

The international channel, on the other hand, relies on the link between the exchange rate and changes in exports and imports. As interest rates are lowered, the exchange rate is not unaffected. Since local prices are responsive to local interest rates, the terms of trade tilt in favor of exporters. A weakening of the local currency affects – at least in the short term – a positive stimulus in the form of an increase in exporters' foreign earnings denominated in domestic currency. It also affects production levels and prices. Of course, the stimulation of exports by currency depreciation is usually not permanent, sometimes it may not even occur at all and be counterproductive right away (it usually is with a lag), since a weakening domestic currency is also a hindered access to international capital. Nota bene, very strong national exporters in the twentieth century were countries that had a very strong currency, stronger even than the dollar (Germany, Japan, Switzerland). Indeed, the lasting strength of exports does not come from short-term manipulation of the exchange rate, but remains significantly dependent on other important factors that promote capital accumulation. However, this does not change the fact that in the short-term model of transmission through the international channel, one can see some reaction in terms of depreciation and its impact on the export sector.

In turn, the last channel of expectations in the transmission is obviously not completely independent. Nota bene all the previous channels are not separate from each other either. When there is a drop in rates and an impact on the real estate sector, for example, we will find both investment and consumption elements in the process, as far as transmission is concerned. And expectations themselves are difficult to separate from any of these categorized transmission channels. Since all sorts of investment decisions, export decisions, consumption decisions are dependent on what expectations actors have about the future, these market expectations are also, in a way, a separate lever influencing how central bank decisions transmit to the economy as a whole. Naturally, lowering interest rates promotes the emergence of expectations associated with the expansionist phase, while raising them introduces an immediate conservative element.

Although concepts of the monetary transmission mechanism have been flourishing for several decades, the value-added in the literature on it is constantly expanding. In addition to neoclassical channels, other channels have begun to appear, in particular the banking channel, the balance sheet channel, and the risk channel (Adrian and Shin 2010; Jiménez et al. 2014; Borio and Zhu 2012; Rajan 2006). All of these auxiliary monetary channels stem from the limitations of formal macroeconomic models that overlook the fact that credit expansion does not occur solely through traditional neoclassical functional responses of market actors.

The capital channel of banks represents the dependence on the portfolio they build. Of course, it cannot be fully separated from the investment and consumption channel, but it is an additional decision point that one takes into account in modeling monetary policy. The banks themselves implement their choices based not only on the investment functions from the IS-LM models. Moreover, it is worth noting here the legal factor, namely banks' capital regulations. The limits and possibilities of credit expansion are not based only on the three classical exogenous tools of the central bank (bound by reserves), and should not even be based on them. Commercial banks' involvement is constrained by the Basel regulations, which determine the ratio of equity capital to risk-weighted assets. In this way, there can even be a merging of monetary transmission with fiscal policy (when, for example, financial supervision forces banks to invest more in specific government bonds perceived as supposedly less risky). The significant impact of regulation on credit expansion may also be due to its static nature. Monetary policy affects banks' profits, albeit through interest rates themselves, which will alter capital levels directly regulating lending decisions (Van den Heuvel 2002, p. 260).

The balance sheet channel, on the other hand, is very similar to banking, but involves the rest of the macroeconomic market. A sizable portion of lending is based on the ability to borrow through collateral offered by market participants. During the boom and lower interest rates, many investment projects have a higher current valuation, which in effect shows up in today's valuation of securities that are used as collateral for loans. In turn, this paves the way for further financing and expanded lending. Since the collateral is able to cover a higher level of debt, the temptation is to take advantage of it. We are familiar with a similar mechanism on the consumption function side, when the rising value of a mortgage can allow further indebtedness and the use of funds generated by the banking system in response.

A significant change in the approach to the monetary transmission mechanism is also related to the phenomenon of the Great Financial Recession and the process of regulatory arbitrage that took place years before it occurred. This is, of course, a situation in which banks transferred new funds not through traditional money creation, but using special purpose vehicles that channeled them into the shadow banking sector (Jabłecki and Machaj 2009; Sieroń 2015, 2017). This, moreover, affected the balance sheets and financing of all entities in any way connected to the financial sector. Consequences were due to two aspects. First, it reduced banks' dependence on traditional financing. Thanks to such changes, from the banks' perspective, it was possible to partially retreat from the classic reliance on the interbank lending market and the need for the other party to accept deposits (which is linked to the reserves and costs involved). Second, it made seemingly illiquid instruments, pinned to specific local markets (such as the local real estate market), suddenly become highly liquid instruments, in some cases almost internationally marketable. In fact, this is how, with the help of good management, it was possible to turn an investment of an illiquid debtor into a very liquid paper based on it. All due to new risk management opportunities that are not apparent in the neoclassical view, which focuses on the functions of investment, export, and consumption.

This qualitative change in the accounts has led the literature to distinguish yet another additional channel of transmission: called the risk channel by Borio and Zhu (2012). What was the reason for this need, and why cannot it be included in the banking or balance sheet channel? Well, empirical estimations are pointed out, which show emphatically that a lower interest rate produces an effect further than just an adaptation of the banking and balance sheet channel. Just as previously the neoclassical channel was not able to account for what is not seen in the investment function, and the banking and balance sheet channel was needed, the analogy is with the adjustment after the risk of the investments made. With reduced interest rates, there is excessive risk on the part of the banks, which is not only due to the balance sheet change but is all the more apparent that less equity capital is involved. As a result, such banks expect less meeting collateral requirements from risky companies, thus shifting the entire spectrum of financial risk (Jiménez et al. 2014). The risk channel, of course, also has an international aspect (Bruno and Shin 2013).

Regardless of which channel of transmission one looks at, it is always the real impact of monetary policy on economic variables that comes from the ability of central banks to create reserves. The central bank's modus operandi is similar to that of any other monopolist: it can target a selected quantity of the good it trades and then have no influence over its price, or it can target a certain price and then have no influence on the quantity. We already know that, for important macroeconomic reasons, the central bank, as a monopolist in the production of final and perfectly liquid means of payment, has let go of targeting specific quantities of the "goods" that it produces. Instead, it targets specific prices of this good (interest rates), providing such sufficient quantities of it (reserves) that the price target is met. In other words, although the quantity of money is not in the final target, it affects the variables in real terms precisely through the channels of monetary transmission. The reduction in rates nominally moves gradually from open market operations and spills over into various markets as is meticulously described by the monetary transmission mechanism literature. This mechanism could not have happened were it not for the central bank's ability to create a monetary base and the entire financial architecture that allows commercial banks to create deposits to secure previously generated loans.

Thus, it can be said that the money supply is found subliminally in any monetary transmission model. For understandable reasons, it may be omitted from the modeling, but this neither means that it is absent, nor that it does not play a causal role in increasing prices with a policy of lowering interest rates. The controversy over the quantity theory of money often flares up precisely because of this issue. There are authors who believe that ignoring the quantity of money means undermining the quantity theory altogether (Alvarez et al. 2001). This applies both to sentimentalists towards the quantity theory and harsh critics, according to whom it has no place in modern macroeconomics. Meanwhile, both extreme approaches lack sufficiently strong justification. Monetary policy may not pay direct attention to money, but that does not mean money is not there. Money is there as a somewhat absentee landlord.

The widespread approach to modern monetary policy in the twenty-first century thus ignores the exchange equation and focuses on other variables. In a now-classic treatise on the subject, Woodford (2003) at one time referred to such newer approaches to monetary policy as "neo-Wicksellian": when, instead of the growth path of monetary aggregates, it focuses on intertemporal spending decisions, thus creating a cashless economy, as it were. Wicksell himself operated with the concepts of interest rates, natural interest rates, real nominal interest rates and the market adaptation that comes with their fluctuations (Wicksell 1962). In his description of the interest rate gap (the divergence of the natural rate from the market rate), he jumps almost immediately to allocation decisions and final prices. Money does not play a priority role there. In this respect, he can indeed be considered the godfather of the modern approach.

Three fundamental equations that determine the most important variables in the model become crucial in such a view (Woodford 2008, pp. 1566–1567). The first links the inflation rate in different periods to real natural output. The second presents the intertemporal relationship of the IS curve, in a way separating spending at different points in time (any change in nominal rates causes spending adaptations over time). The third equation, in turn, defines a monetary policy rule, somewhat related to the previous two. The third one could, for example, be a Taylor rule, in which the central bank operates its short-term rates in such a way as to balance the levels of inflation and the output gap simultaneously, with parameters assigned to them, giving the appropriate weight. Some of the variables are treated exogenously in this situation, and therefore as a given in advance. What is characteristic of such a framework is that it does not refer directly to the amount of money in circulation. Inflation itself is basically determined by the central bank's inflation target and the current and future differences between the natural rate of interest in combination with the central bank's response adaptation function. The goal seems to have been achieved: the leading monetary determinant in the economy, that is, the inflation rate, is modeled using interest rates and without using the quantity of money.

It is not the end of the story, however, as Woodford does not take a position entirely in opposition to quantity theory. At the same time, he points out that following monetary policy rules that are based on interest rates could also imply long-term stable growth of the money supply, while there is no monitoring of this growth geared to the implementation of the rule (Woodford 2008, p. 1572). So the relationship between money and prices would not be excluded, and could even be the invisible core of such a model. As he points out transparently, the exchange equation itself (money spent equals money received) does not contradict the fundamental variables of New Keynesian models. Not that seldom descriptions of the effects of monetary policy in the New Keynesian models are made with an emphasis on changes in monetary aggregates (e.g. Zimmerman 2003). The quantity of money simply changes alongside interest rates in such a situation as the central bank implements interest rate rules (Woodford 2008, p. 1573). Such consistency and translation of the money supply into prices at a ratio of almost 1 to 1 can occur in either model. At the same time, this additional equation of exchange is not necessary to predict the evolution of inflation, output and rates in the economy under a given central bank rate rule. Therefore, it must be strongly emphasized that adopting the Neo-Wicksellian framework of fundamental equations without the exchange equation does not mean rejecting the quantity theory of money. Rather, it is an approach from a different angle and with the omission of a certain mechanistic description. Classical monetarism focuses on empirical and reasonably simple correlations between key macroeconomic aggregates, while the structural estimations used by the New Keynesian inspiration are a search for a different model. One need not automatically exclude the other.

All in all, against the backdrop of the prevailing critical, or at least reserved, approach to quantity theory, Woodford has shown himself to be, on balance anyway, lightly in favor of recognizing the quantity theory of money. In his polemic, Nelson (2008) goes much further and points out that it is not only that the exchange equation can be reconciled with the structural equation in modern monetary policy. He recognizes that the exchange equation is even a necessary assumption in such equations, which are de facto implicit in the assumption of controlling long-term interest rates. Nelson discusses here a "high-level assumption," which boils down to the fact of steady-state inflation rate as an instrument in the long run with output and real interest rates both equal in the longer run to their steady-state natural values. Under those conditions, the inflation rate and nominal money growth have a one-to-one long-run relationship. Henceforth not only is the quantity theory perfectly compatible with equations spelled out by Woodford, but even more: they are a necessary part of them (Nelson 2008, p. 1803).

Nelson then points out how the real effects of monetary policy work in the model described by Woodford, and they, too, fall within the monetary transmission mechanism, resulting de facto from the creation of additional money. In the short run, deviations from monetary neutrality (no one-to-one translation of money into prices) are due to temporary nominal rigidities (at least with Woodford and New Keynesianism, which can also be argued with). As a result of partial price adjustments, open market operations do not trigger an immediate response of the entire price index, and thus not only nominal cash balances change, but also real balances. In the long run, on the other hand, adaptation takes place, nominal rigidity disappears completely, and monetary neutrality returns, in which prices move as much as the aggregate money supply. The determination of real balances is detached from nominal determination, the liquidity effect fades away (Nelson 2008, p. 1804). Somewhat supportive of Nelson's point of view Caraiani (2016) makes an argument that macroeconomic predictions are improved if DSGE models (used by the central bank) are improved by taking money into account.

In the end, therefore, not only is there no clash between quantity theory and more contemporary descriptions of the monetary transmission mechanism, but there is rather a harmony between the effects of the money supply on final prices and the real effects on interest rates. When a central bank targets interest rates, it must generate some means of payment to do so. No other entity is able to do this to the same extent. Going further up the banking hierarchy, when a commercial bank extends some credit, it must do so by simultaneously generating some deposit. Thus, targeting a certain level of interest rate can do so through the power of bank money creation. Otherwise, that is, without such money creation, it would actually have to raise money from some other source, and then the story of banks as pure financial intermediaries would be true (I discuss this more in the next chapter). They would become a chain linking recipients of investment capital with someone who lends capital as a saver. Both expansionary central bank and commercial bank policies can be carried out thanks to the fact that some money supply is created. This makes a nominal reduction in interest rates as much as possible a real reduction. In other words, the money trail is essentially inescapable in the mechanics of monetary transmission. The central bank sets the desired size of the interest rate through open market operations that determine the money supply, even if the money supply is determined from monetary demand: but *it is*, even if it does not appear in the central bank's optimal monetary rule (Beck and Wieland, p. 528).

As Mervyn King (2002) summarized the situation, although all economic deliberations are usually about money, they often leave out the concept of money directly. This is no different with macroeconomics and central bank policies, which focus their messages mainly on interest rates – and for good reason, since, as we have seen, monetary increments affect real variables through transmission channels. At the same time, the withdrawal or disappearance of the money supply from modeling does not mean that its relationship with prices does not exist. For it is as real as it can be, only it occurs in a complex system in which simple transmission is not easy to measure, is distorted by many other factors, and does not occur immediately, but with some delay. All the more so because we are also talking about a situation in which in the short term the leading role is played by the expectations of market players, which are not determined in advance by any hard variables, but are based on subjective perception of macroeconomic reality.

5 Active monetary policy after 2008 and the inadequacy of the money multiplier model

2008 remains the most important macroeconomic event of the twenty-first century for many reasons. First, at that time we were dealing with the greatest economic crisis since the Great Depression, which received its own name: the Great Financial Recession. Secondly, it saw the launch of unprecedented modern monetary policy tools, which had previously been presented mainly in theoretical studies and soon were to become not-so-unconventional (Claeys 2014). The situation was also interesting in that the practitioner who put them into practice was the previously respected theorist of these interventions, namely Ben Bernanke (Bernanke and Reinhart 2004). The rationale for them was mainly inspired by Milton Friedman's empirical studies in the case of the Great Depression. This is because the idea was to avoid a decline in the money supply (Bernanke 2002). Yet what was analyzed by Bernanke was actually not the money supply, but the financial deleveraging that comes with its decline. In principle, the post-2008 interventions can be thought of more as a way to reverse financial deleveraging with less emphasis on what exactly will happen to the monetary aggregates. Because of this seemingly subtle difference completely dissimilar predictions have been born about what would happen to inflation after such programs.

The theoretical articles of the later Nobel laureate pointed out how to get out of the supposed monetary policy trap, when, during a crisis, the central bank using classical intervention tools reaches a wall and is unable to effectively push the monetary transmission mechanism. This trap is characterized by reaching virtually zero nominal central bank interest rates, which do not significantly translate into the behavior of economic agents as traditionally modeled transmission predicts. The monetary transmission mechanism was broken down. Reduced interest rates had no effect on market rates – or looking from the monetary side, additional (and cheaper) reserves in the banking system did not have the expected monetary effect.

DOI: 10.4324/9781003432562-5

Bernanke mentioned three important methods of intervening in such a situation. The first concerned managing the expectations of market players. The central bank was to consistently send signals to the market environment that its interventions were not short-term in nature and would continue for several quarters. Generally speaking, there is usually a maturity mismatch between central bank-controlled rates and market rates – and quite a large one, ranging from several weeks to several decades. Bonds issued by central banks have short maturities, while commercial banks finance long-term assets, sometimes mortgages as long as forty years. Market players thus have reasons to treat with ease any central bank interventions with long-term expectations of a return to higher rates. Not just on a scale of years, but even quarters. This first emergency tool actually serves to combat such expectations playing on the return of higher rates. Hence, since the end of 2008, virtually every Federal Reserve announcement has contained the same repeated message: interest rates are low and will remain low for the next few quarters, so there is no reason to build expectations for a restrictive monetary policy in the near term. In the first phase, such communications seemed not to be spectacularly successful, but over time the market began to accept this approach as the new extraordinary standard.

The second tool is quantitative easing notoriously mentioned in the popular press, that is, the extraordinary (in terms of its size) increase in commercial banks' reserves in the system that occurred with the gigantic expansion of the central bank's balance sheet. The central bank began to accept more willingly in open market operations financial assets acquired from private banks. This played an important role in the market for these assets, stemming market corrections, and naturally improving the overall balance sheet situation of the commercial banks. Having additional reserves in exchange for problem assets means that a bank's balance sheet situation improves. As a last resort, the bank's reserves can simply be placed at the central bank and additional funds can be obtained from them, bypassing the challenges and uncertainties associated with the commercial assets market. This option is all the more attractive when even the mandatory reserves are interest-bearing.

The third tool is related to the second (although it is not quite the same thing) and involves qualitative easing. Not only is the central bank to expand its activism in the market for financial assets, but it is also to sharply lower its standards for the quality of the securities it accepts. This applies to both the risk associated with them and their maturity. The second of these issues has come to be known as "operation twist," with the swapping of short-term papers for long-term ones. The first of these issues meant, for example, deeper involvement in the market for securities linked to low-quality commercial loans, which the market had begun to perceive as junk and heading for a radical downward valuation adjustment. The twist operation came in the later phase of central bank intervention, when fiscal intervention was in full swing alongside monetary policy, requiring monetization of public debt. The first phase of the crisis, on the other hand, was a kind of "shortage" of government paper, which commercial banks were very eager to take on their balance sheets. Essentially, this was done in exchange for risky commercial paper, which in turn landed on the central bank's balance sheet – so the term "qualitative" easing is very apt here. The swelling balance sheet of the lender of last resort took place at the same time with a lower quality balance sheet. Therefore, the two operations were, in total, like a single tool, but this is not always necessary. One can imagine a situation in which the central bank increases its balance sheet, but in its entirety only to support the fiscal channel. Then it would inject additional reserves into the system, but only to finance the increased public debt and expand the conduct of fiscal policy. Therefore, it is theoretically possible to disentangle the two.

All three tools are essentially a kind of declaration of war against yield curves: the one showing time spreads and the one showing risk spreads. As I indicated above, traditional central bank operations only affect the initial shape of these two curves. In the case of time-related because they involve weeks (compared to banks' investments calculated in years), in the case of risk-related because they involve the safest securities (usually government). The extraordinary tool Bernanke wrote about is supposed to abandon these limitations and thus allow much more influence on market players. In effect, entering this sphere to "fix" the monetary transmission mechanism essentially means changing the nature of the "lender of last resort." In the classical sense, the central bank intervenes to improve the liquidity of financial entities. With such advanced tools, it begins to improve the de facto profitability of businesses, not just their liquidity.

Undoubtedly, all of these interventions had a significant impact on what happened to the US economy in the following years, but the interpretation of these interventions when they occurred left a great deal of inaccuracy (though it certainly boosted credit markets, see for example, Haldane et al. 2016; and government assets, see Joyce et al. 2011). The popular press and commentators treated these extraordinary tools as a classic money-creation mechanism that would spill over record inflation into the dollar economy. What's more, some of the popular commentators even suggested that this could end in inflation of several tens of percent, or even hyperinflation and a collapse of the dollar along the lines of the Weimar Republic.

Indeed, such risk perceptions were a litmus test, recognizing whether or not one was more deeply versed in the meanderings of monetary policy. In essence, however, such concerns were not completely divorced from economics. Such hypothetical reasoning was based on the classic textbook description of money supply growth exogenously orchestrated by a central control entity. It was supposed to look exactly as many textbooks incorrectly say it does to this day: the central bank conducts very aggressive open market operations, accepts poor-quality paper and injects more reserves into commercial banks. The banks can now "use" these reserves and thereby create more deposits to (partially) cover them, and then pass them on to customers in the form of loans. Everything was supposed to work harmoniously according to the money creation multiplier. If, simplistically, reserves for deposits are 5 percent, the bank can generate another 20 dollars in bank deposits from every additional dollar from the Federal Reserve. The record overgrowth of the monetary base is presented in Figure 5.1.

Here we also see a partial reason why quantity theory of money was being neglected is the case of huge monetary interventions after the Great Financial Crisis of 2008. While Ben Bernanke was introducing his innovative monetary policy tools, the monetary base has more than doubled, a startling increase which has not been seen in the United States. Usually, most hyperinflations happen when such base money expansion is being triggered (although there are some exceptions to this rule: for example in Weimar Republic banks' money was expanding faster than base money). That is the reason that leads some commentators to make a predictive statement that the US economy is heading towards double-digit inflation, sometimes even on the verge of regular hyperinflation.

The multiplier theory states that banks first and foremost accumulate sources of financing and then seek opportunities to allocate them. In this, they are to resemble financial intermediaries (see for example, Hellwig 2000; Heffernan 1996; Diamond and Rajan 2001; Kashyap et al. 2002; Gertler and Kiyotaki 2010; Stein 2014). In the loanable funds market, they can either raise savings in the form of time deposits (or bonds, etc.) or in the form of on-demand deposits. Putting these funds together, they then choose where to allocate them depending on the expected profitability of the investment. If this description correctly reflects the functioning of modern banks, then indeed the reserves injected by central banks open the way for the creation of more deposits and loans. These, in turn, are almost passively supposed to respond to this.

If such a mechanical-exogenous theory of money generation is true, the doubling of the monetary base does look worrying for future inflation levels. What's more, these concerns could easily fit coherently into the central bank's intervention plans: it was about qualitative and quantitative easing, sending a clear signal about them so that the level of lending – and consequently spending in the economy – would not fall. Putting these factors together, it comes out that very high inflation should have appeared soon.

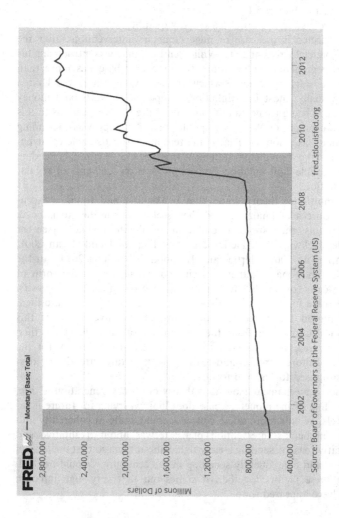

Figure 5.1 Monetary base in the United States (2001–2012).

Source: St. Louis Federal Reserve.

The mechanical banking prism has been verified by subsequent macroeconomic experience with no high inflation at all. However, even before the appearance (or non-appearance) of these consequences, it was to be expected that very high inflation was not at all imminent, since the extraordinary tools of monetary policy were designed to mainly bail out the banking sector. All three interventions – signaling an inflationary course, increasing the central bank's balance sheet, and worsening its quality – were designed to inch up commercial banks' balance sheets. It was a cleaning of the banks' books to avoid a banking and financial disaster. Junk assets ceased to weigh so heavily on private books and were shifted to the public books, in central bank accounts. The first effects of such interventions meant that commercial banks were better off in terms of their capital ratio: more direct reserves and safer (government) paper on the books. Even from a regulatory standpoint, this meant a significant improvement.

On the other hand, soiling the central bank's books and transferring any nominal losses (which did not occur anyway) to the somewhat public sector was not a problem for the latter. The central bank does not have classical capital. It can operate on negative capital without major problems. And it can even, with such operations – along with a sufficiently strong inflationary increase – show subsequent "profits", resulting from jacking up the prices of purchased assets (which, by the way, occurred in later years).

The key point in the whole operation is that such balance sheet swapping (from private banks to the central bank) took place with an explosion of bank reserves, but at the same time was not followed by a further expansion of broader aggregates, as there was a recessionary correction of investment mistakes in the market. Or, to use Richard Koo's terminology, we had a balance sheet recession, during which lenders looked for prudent capital management anyway, rather than further exploration and deepening of risky investments (Koo 2001, 2010, 2012, 2014).

As a result, these extraordinary interventions by Bernanke – while they may have halted declines in the money supply – did not at the same time lead to such radical increases in the money supply as occurred in the case of the monetary base. The mechanism of impact was different, as the central bank's interventions provided commercial banks with additional bank reserves, but these were not used for further increased credit and deposit generation. This is well reflected in Figure 5.2.

Increases in the monetary aggregate M2 have of course occurred, thanks also to the radical increase in M0, but it is difficult to speak of a spectacular imitation here. Indeed, the pivot beyond the earlier trend is barely noticeable. Naturally, one may ask a legitimate question as to why exactly I chose the M2 money supply indicator. This is not

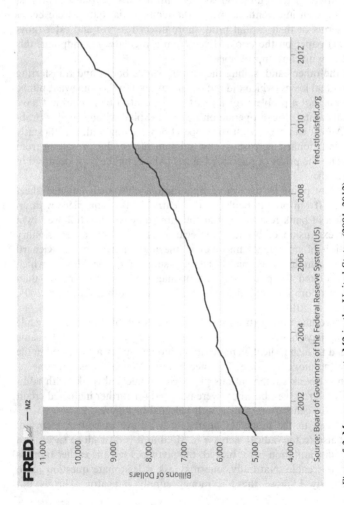

Figure 5.2 Money aggregate M2 in the United States (2001–2012).
Source: St. Louis Federal Reserve.

particularly relevant to illustrate the point. We could just as well have used the M1, M2A, or M3 indicator. The key effect would be similar despite some differences: the jump in the monetary base did not translate in the same way into jumps in the broader monetary aggregates. The hockey stick was not really intended to translate into the overall economy with radical increments in the amount of money in circulation. Its tasks were different from the start.

This mismatch between the growth of M0 and domestic money may be difficult – if not impossible – to explain with the classic textbook approach to the money creation multiplier. However, it is not a challenge if we treat broad money as generated by a whole set of various interacting banking and economic factors. Or if we treat money at least in part as the concept of endogeneity of money suggests. Commercial banks do not first accumulate reserves and deposits from other customers to then become intermediaries of that capital in transferring it to borrowers (Jakab and Kumhof 2015, Disyatat 2010). Thus, they do not fulfill the function of coordinating the money and loan market. They do not balance among themselves previously accumulated "savings" with "investments" the way it looks in the scheme of loan funds. Of course, banks are happy to raise additional cheaper capital in the form of free reserves or from interested customers with which they will issue corporate bonds. But that does not mean automation on the asset side and funding lending. Rather, from this angle, banks look for profit opportunities by assessing the profitability of a given lending project (weighted by risk and some formula of uncertainty) against the broader costs of trying to implement it. Simplifying the matter a bit, since assets show what banks own and liabilities show where they got it from, profit-seeking activity means a spectrum of considerations about what else to own and where to get the funds for it.

In endogenous terms, this means that if banks see a good credit project, they can finance it by generating broad monetary aggregates at a given interest rate, and with them the deposits needed to do so – popularly speaking, "out of thin air," although not "out of thin air at ease" (at creation they convert future paying capacity into current liquid deposits). To carry out these projects, they may have current funds, they may have excess liquid reserves, and if they do not have them, they can simply borrow them from elsewhere – naturally from other banks, or from the central bank, if necessary. This costs money, of course, but it is this cost that is key, not the amount of reserves themselves. That is why reserves alone do not automatically translate into broad money aggregates. Rather, what matters is the cost of these reserves – of possibly holding them, possibly investing them, or possibly acquiring them. The facts are that specific reserve levels are not the central bank's goal. The specific target is inflation paired according to models with levels of nominal interest rates.

For this reason, the multiplier description misses the mark, despite the fact that it is still taught today in the first years of the studies of future economists. Not surprisingly in view of this, those who do not get directly into the factual analysis of the monetary system are tempted to see the growth of the monetary base as a warning signal for automatically record inflation. Part of the educational role in this regard has been played by the central banks themselves, in particular by the publications of the Bank of England (2014) and Bundesbank (2017), which have attempted to reach economic popularizers and investment news sources (see also Goodhart 1989).

In his landmark 2014 text, Werner actually went even further in his description, as he returned to the popularized formulation that banks create deposits "out of thin air." This was based on his empirical description showing that when banks generate loans, there are no transfers of current deposits between departments of banks. These funds are simply created when a loan tranche is released. If someone takes out a mortgage to buy an apartment, the bank simply transfers money to the account of the owner of the apartment, who sells it. And in the course of this transfer, a new deposit is created, which was nowhere to be found before. Hence the term "out of thin air" seems to be popularly accurate – some purchasing power that did not exist before is generated. Of course, it is not the case that these resources are created without any restrictions. The term can perniciously imply this. Since something is created almost at the snap of the fingers, in principle there is nothing to prevent it from being replicated without limitation. Such is not the case when a credit-creating commercial bank faces key constraints that will force it to be disciplined in creating funds ex nihilo. What is more, the creation of funds ex nihilo is not done so that banks directly benefit from it, since banks do not create new funds for themselves, but create new funds in order to lend them out at a profit and earn from it.

Thus, we can see why the post-2008 period did not end in very high inflation, let alone hyperinflation. For our purpose, the most important issue to discuss at the end remains how the failure of the mechanistic concept of the money creation multiplier relates to the concept of the quantity theory of money. In principle, very similar to how it was in the previously discussed case, the Friedman program. Although one supports the other, they are not the same thing. Just as the quantity theory of money does not require the veracity and sensibility of Friedman's program, exactly the same is true of the multiplier concept of exogenous money. Quantity theory says that increases in the money supply exert inflationary pressures on prices and in the long run cause nominal adjustments. And this is true regardless of how this money supply grows and the exact mechanism behind it. The money supply can also grow as described by the endogenous money tradition. Deposits can be created by banks out of thin air and usually without mechanistically looking at the reserves available to do so. Banks may not be intermediaries at all in the financial market (Jakab and Kumhof 2015). However, nothing prevents the money so created by the banking system from having an effect on nominal prices consistent with the description of the quantity theory of money. Quantity theory does not require that money remains under the perfect control of the central bank. The central bank could just as well have absolutely no control over how much money is in each monetary aggregate. This, of course, is not the case, but even if this hypothetically were the case, the principle of the translation of the long-run of these monetary aggregates into final prices may still apply.

Paul Krugman suggested in an interview that the quantity theory of money has failed as a theoretical construct because increased levels of inflation did not emerge after the application of extraordinary monetary policy tools in 2008. In reality, however, this is a failure on the part of the mechanistic model of money creation, which, nota bene, is not necessarily consistent with the quantity theory of money either. It is possible to imagine someone who recognizes the model of exogenous money, growing in proportion to the reserves injected into the banks, and at the same time recognizing that this does not cause inflationary pressure. Recognizing the correctness of the simple multiplier concept of money creation does not require recognizing the quantity theory of money, nor, conversely, recognizing the incorrectness of the multiplier concept does not mean rejecting the quantity theory. The options for combinations of claims about these things are really more than two. The confusion of these issues seems somewhat natural, for the reason that many who warned of high inflation in 2008 after Bernanke's launch of the tools, used a simplified multiplier model. They were certainly wrong in this, but this in no way undermines the quantity theory. The story is the same as it was with the Friedman program.

Moreover, if one were to look closely at the data for the period after 2008, then in light of the quantity theory of money, inflation should not have reached record levels after these interventions! If this had happened, if inflation had reached record levels befitting the rate of growth of the monetary base, then we could talk about a possible falsification of the quantity theory of money. For then it would turn out that record double-digit inflation without increases in broad monetary aggregates had occurred. The opposite of what quantity theory predicts, since no one accepts the nineteenth-century approach to the definition of money, according to which only the monetary base would be money. We know that most transactions in the economy are handled with bank money, so something broader than M0 must surely appear in the exchange equation. Meanwhile, after 2008, everything happened as predicted by the quantity theory: since money supply growth did not significantly break out above standard trends, final inflation rates did not do so either. Nota bene completely different from the pandemic years, that is, from 2020 onward.

Quantity theory of money, at its core, has a very unambiguous message that has its macroeconomic relevance to theories of economic growth and development – that nominal increases in money in circulation have a long-term effect primarily on nominal prices. This, however, does not mean that it can be easily used to predict future macroeconomic variables. The case is true of all three things discussed so far: (1) Friedman's program to easily manage inflation by controlling the quantity of money, (2) the long-run statistical relationship between prices and inflation levels, which breaks down at lower levels, (3) the money creation multiplier discussed here, which was to be used to describe the exogenous monetary impact on final prices in the case of the extraordinary interventions implemented after the Great Financial Recession. None of these three things is required for the quantity theory of money to be true.

If one can indulge in an interdisciplinary analogy here, it might be interesting to compare the quantity theory of money to the concept of caloric balance in the nutritional sciences. In these sciences, it is clear that an increased caloric intake triggers a tendency toward fat accumulation, while a reduction in caloric intake triggers a tendency toward fat reduction. But this does not mean that a change in caloric intake can always be easily quantitatively translated into adipose tissue, since it would also be necessary to strictly control the body's caloric expenditure, including resting metabolism, which may secondarily depend on the amount of calories consumed (and for that depend on non-resting metabolism). In all of this, complex metabolic, neurological, and hormonal reactions come into consideration, which indirectly affect how many calories are consumed, how they are digested and how they are spent. Moreover – when it comes to the pragmatics of weight loss and lifestyle change programs, simply counting calories consumed and calories spent is one of the worst ways to lose body mass. It is extremely difficult to do, and the literature clearly shows that there are other and much more effective ways to achieve this goal (for example, changing the diet in terms of quality or using pharmacotherapy). For most people, it is better to forget about counting calories at all when aiming for a certain body weight and follow a program that skips that. But this in no way changes the fact that while pursuing such strategies a person somewhat unknowingly achieves a caloric deficit without performing calorie calculations. People losing body fat can do this effectively without counting calories spent and calories absorbed.

De facto quantity theory of money can be viewed in a similar way. Lowering inflation most often requires the appearance of a reduction in significant increments in the money supply. Higher inflation most often requires the appearance of increments in the money supply. But that does not mean that an effective strategy is to actually measure, monitor, and target monetary aggregates. It is quite likely that – in an environment of central banking and a macroeconomically stable economy – there are other ways to achieve direct inflation targeting than measuring the amount of money in circulation. As we know, this is mainly done by targeting certain levels of nominal interest rates. Then, if the model is well adjusted to reality, it may just turn out that the money supply reaches such levels that allow for stable inflation. Even if the monetary committees have not looked at what the size of the monetary aggregates are. Unless a situation arises in which the monetary aggregates are so ignored that they shoot up above traditional increments in the background without due attention. This is exactly what happened in the pandemic era.

6 Active monetary policy during the 2020 pandemic

We come to the finale of our story about the quantity theory of money, which confirmed its relevancy through the example of active monetary policy during the epidemic. We have seen that over the past several decades, this relevancy has never really been lost, and no challenge it has faced has directly addressed it. On the other hand, since high inflation was relevant to previous generations, quantity theory could actually be set aside somewhere and, in some cases of macroeconomic modeling, simply forgotten (as we have seen, mainly due to monetary transmission models and the relatively successful direct inflation targeting strategy). Until 2020 happened.

The pandemic or epidemic effect on inflation levels itself appears to be ambiguous. On the one hand, aggregate analysis may suggest that inflation will fall as a result of epidemics, while on the other hand, the opposite is true. At the end of 2021, a study was published that indicated that in Europe, epidemics tend to make inflation lower (Bonam and Smadu 2021). At least that is what the data collected from the fourteenth to the twentieth century suggested.

However, the authors were far from suggesting a repetition of a similar course of events, as evidenced by the very title of the study: will this time be different? In the article's conclusion, they point out that the reactions of governments this time are unprecedented and could end up being the opposite of the previous trend. However, the article lacked an analysis of the monetary element, moreover, in line with the current paradigm of ignoring money. Yet at least it highlighted the risks of inflation. Some of the articles did not mention anything about inflation issues, despite touching on the macroeconomic consequences of the epidemic (e.g., Eichenbaum et al. 2021).

Another study (Brzoza-Brzezina et al. 2021) undertook a price-forming analysis without the monetary aggregates. The authors pointed out that in the epidemic there are two effects in opposite directions according to the monetary transmission mechanism: in the labor market

DOI: 10.4324/9781003432562-6

and in the consumption market, which is derived from the real action of government intervention (i.e. lockdowns). As a result, on the price-generating side, little could be said in advance other than the altogether Wittgensteinian prediction that inflation could theoretically go either way (rise, fall, or stay the same). In the end, inflation went down slightly in the first phase of the epidemic, before rising for good from 2021 onward. The authors note that in a laissez-faire scenario, inflation would remain flat, as both the labor market and consumption would adjust to a similar extent, making aggregate levels even. However, this analysis, like many others, makes no mention of monetary aggregates. Indeed, the word "money" appears zero times in it.

Another study (Lepetit et al. 2021) pointed out that monetary policy tends to be rather ineffective during epidemics compared to normal times, as households adjust their behavior autonomously between periods depending on their risk of falling ill. As a result, lowering real interest rates through traditional channels is less effective in propping up economic activity. This analysis also did not focus on the effect of nominal money supply growth. It juxtaposed the trade-off between price stability and minimizing distortions from infection externalities.

English et al. (2021) interpreted the epidemic situation as a repeat of the earlier years of reaching the zero-bound interest rate wall. The 2020 situation was interpreted as a typical case of extreme Knightian uncertainty, which allegedly again required extraordinary interventions by monetary authorities. Central banks around the world undertook interventions that varied, but were essentially the following operations, which were already familiar. First, significant reductions in interest rates combined with forward guidance to stimulate aggregate demand. Second, financial market asset purchase programs were launched. Third, liquidity operations and credit support (lending to financial firms) were provided. Often in combination with government support. And fourth, regulatory easing was also carried out, that is, traditional capital and liquidity buffers were let go.

Meanwhile, let us take a look at what happened to the US money supply during the epidemic, particularly against the backdrop of what occurred during the Great Financial Recession. Let's start with the rate of growth of the monetary base in Figure 6.1.

If one were to suggest a comparison to the 2008 approach, then indeed an attitude suggesting no inflationary threat seems quite reasonable. The scare of high inflation doesn't seem out of place during an epidemic, since the monetary base increments during the Great Financial Recession were even larger, and yet we didn't end up with high price increases. However, we know that the quantity theory of money is not based on a multiplier concept, so we should analyze the growth rate of some broader monetary aggregate. In this case, let us take the M2 indicator shown in Figure 6.2.

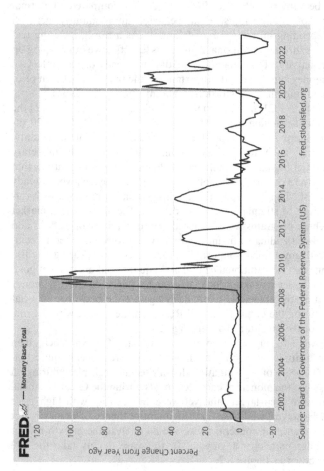

Figure 6.1 Percent growth of monetary base in the United States, monthly percent change compared to year earlier 2000–2023. (From Federal Reserve St Louis.)

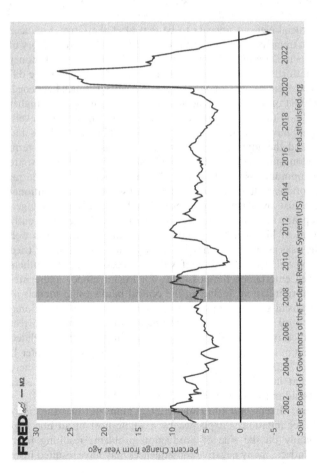

Figure 6.2 Percent growth of money supply M2 in the United States, monthly percent change compared to year earlier 2000–2023. (From Federal Reserve St Louis.)

The difference between monetary policy during the pandemic and what went before is becoming evident. The rate of growth of the monetary aggregate M2 is not only far greater than the post-2008 period, but is a record for the entire twenty-first century. Such record growth rates, moreover, were not even in the last 20 years of the twentieth century. So it can be said straightforwardly that the tools of monetary intervention have been set in motion, and they have done much to shake the US economy out of state X and push it on a path toward state Y, where the impact of the monetary aggregate on final inflation levels begins to materialize. Burdekin (2020) was among those who recognized that monetary developments after 2020 were not the same as in 2008 after the crises. Changing reserves was not the only thing. Other monetary developments started to happen. Kantor (2022) discusses these aspects ex post, showing again why the post-pandemic events unfolded in a much different way than after 2008. The crucial element appears to be that after the Great Financial Recession, an immense balance sheet pressure existed. Quantity theory of money always relied on the notion of monetary demand, not just money supply. Henceforth with huge financial deleveraging, 2008 had to be different from post-pandemic economy, where no financial crunch happened.

Pinter (2021) on the other hand has made an argument that higher money supply, in this case, should not translate into higher price levels, because higher money balances are to be "absorbed" by individuals and companies, and the adjustments are expected to arise in a longer-term horizon – alongside the fact that exceptional increases in money are probably temporary also with a possible exit strategy by the central bank. The options include increases in the interest rates by conventional methods, but also by balance sheet reversal (selling bonds in exchange). Well, it appears that the case was not so easy, and the apparently unlikely event of higher inflation did happen. Pinter at least was well aware of the risks associated with the monetary side of the issue and tried to comprehensively address it (even if without success). But many others have not even entertained the possibility for higher money aggregates leading to more inflation. Including the central banks using models of monetary transmission without money. Henceforth the international chorus of central banks has made strikingly and uniformly incorrect inflation predictions around the world. Mistakes impressively correlated with the extent of additional monetary growth as discussed in Chapter 1. Hendrickson (2023) made a point that even before the pandemic there were signs that including monetary aggregates in quantitative easing programs would make them more "effective" on their own ground.

In addition, Greenwood and Hanke (2022) point out that the emergence of higher inflation is explained by a whole host of ad hoc suggestions, mainly on the side of production problems resulting from lockdowns. Indeed, many negative consequences may have resulted from them in terms of coordination problems in various markets and supply chains. However, it is difficult to explain the existence of a sustained inflationary impulse in virtually all markets. The article cites Jerome Powell's words before Congress, who was asked if the record growth in the M2 monetary aggregate since World War II was showing something. Powell countered that when he studied economics, there was a correlation between this aggregate and economic growth, and now it has no implications for the economic outlook. Moreover, we have allegedly seen sizable increases in the aggregate on several occasions without higher inflation emerging. Two things from the US central bank governor's statement are worth clarifying at this point. First, M2 has never been linked to economic growth. Analyses in the spirit of quantity theory of money have always, including recent studies, shown the absence of a long-term correlation between economic growth and money supply. Second, there may have been systematic increases in monetary aggregates in the past, but after the interventions of the epidemic era, we did not repeat the past, but went much further in record increases in the money supply. This monetary growth really was different.

Of course, it is still possible to use a different language in describing inflationary processes altogether, just as is done with the transmission mechanism. Lapavitsas (2022), for example, argues that the monetary description of pandemics misses the mark, and that post-pandemic inflation can be explained by the turnout of aggregate demand and aggregate supply. Supply would be expected to remain weak, while global demand would increase excessively as a result of intervention tools. Well, this description may be as correct as possible, but subliminally it could also include a monetary mechanism, especially when the real product surpassed the product from pre-pandemic levels, and high inflation still showed up. Indeed, one could, like Werner (2014), ask the question: and where did the relative increase in global demand come from? Did spending on it come entirely from reallocations of pre-existing money? Or was there a coincidental expansion of monetary aggregates and the emergence of new money "out of thin air"?

Conclusions

As we have seen, quantity theory of money has remained a sort of absentee landlord in the macroeconomic world. It has been absent in regular and broad practices of monetary policy models, but this absence was due to visibility, not true causality. Quantity theory was not seen, because most of monetary policy has been down in the realms of the economy type X with low inflation. Despite changing conditions, nothing has changed in macroeconomic research showing correlations between money and final prices. All studies have pointed out that economies are divided into group X, with low inflation and weak correlation, and group Y, with higher inflation, which shows a strong correlation.

At the end of the study, we can separate very different theses that are not mutually exclusive and which, at the same time, do not require full agreement for any of them to be true.

First, the quantity theory of money primarily relies on the thesis that increasing the money supply results in inflationary pressure on prices and has a long-term effect primarily on nominal variables (which does not imply super neutrality).

Second, this does not mean that the money supply is easy to measure or that it is easy to find an ideal empirical indicator of it that would be universally suitable for data analysis in most places and times.

Third, the quantity theory of money does not mean that money is exogenous and that it is under relatively easy control of the central bank. In view of this, it does not mean that the textbook money creation multiplier describes the process of monetary expansion well. Money can be endogenous, or partially endogenous, and at the same time, the total quantity of money can affect inflation levels.

Fourth, the quantity theory of money in no way implies that the money creation multiplier, common in textbooks, captures well the nature of the interdependence of base money and internal money generated by banks. Nor, in view of this, does it imply that reserves are the

DOI: 10.4324/9781003432562-7

primary tool for directing the total money supply. There may just as well be other key (and it appears that there are) tools that influence it.

Fifth, the quantity theory of money does not mean that monetary aggregates must always correlate with inflation rates at all levels. Hence, the de facto absence of such a correlation also does not mean that such a relationship does not exist at all levels.

What was conspicuously missing from the direct implementation of monetary policy in the years after 2020 was the memory that there are X economies and Y economies. The natural consequence of this – the possibility of a smooth transition from state X to state Y as a result of an excessive increase in the money supply in circulation. The lesson of the post-2020 period with record levels of inflation in recent years could therefore be that observing broad aggregates can make sense.

Laurence Meyer (2001) stated "Money plays no role in today's consensus macro model. It plays virtually no role in the conduct of monetary policy, at least in the United States." Gerald Bouey said "We didn't abandon monetary aggregates, they abandoned us," also indicating that monetary aggregates no longer play roles in the conduct of monetary policy (Manoj and Goodhart 2021). Well, it looks like the prodigal son is back.

As we know, there were some theoretical arguments behind this. However (from a monetary policy perspective), there may be some common ground between ignoring money supply indicators altogether and targeting their specific levels. In all likelihood, controlling a specific monetary aggregate is doomed to failure, but that doesn't mean there is no point in paying any attention to them. After all, it may turn out that turning towards them will be a good fuse for noticing the transition from the state of economy X to the state of economy Y, and well in advance, because at the moment of excessive monetary growth. And therefore before it even triggers increases in the final price index.

This view is far from revolutionary and was presented at the turn of the century when turning back on monetary aggregates became a new norm. Right then over 20 years ago, a mundane paper was published. It is worthwhile to quote at length conclusions that could not be any more relevant than they are today:

> Much recent academic literature on monetary policy has suggested that monetary aggregates should not play a large role in monetary policy decisions. Within the so-called new neoclassical synthesis, monetary developments are not seen as playing an active role in the transmission mechanism of monetary policy. Monetary policy rules advocated by adherents of these models are often moneyless – they suggest that central banks can neglect or even ignore monetary developments when making interest rate decisions Moreover, many prominent empirical studies, in particular for the US, have concluded that the demand for money is

unstable in both long and short runs and that monetary developments largely constitute "noise" which policymakers would do well to ignore.
This paper has challenged these very strong – and, in our view, erroneous – conclusions. On empirical grounds, we survey a large literature that supports the view that money has a stable relationship with prices (...).
On empirical and practical grounds, we suggest that monetary developments contain information about the state of the economy which regardless of whether money plays an active role in the transmission mechanism of monetary policy – should be integrated into the policy-making process (Masuch et al. 2004).

As the authors openly stated, "monetary aggregates in monetary policy decisions can provide an important safeguard against major policy mistakes in the presence of model uncertainty." Or to paraphrase using our classification, monetary aggregates can be a safeguard against circumstances in which significant, apparently unpredicted model shifting happens (from X to Y). It may look unpredictable due to the fact that stable parameters of type X economy assume stable parameters and central bank's functions that allow to successfully reach the direction inflation targeting goal (as presented in our discussion with Woodford's approach). Under such circumstances, there may not be possibilities for any spotting the change from X to Y and such evolution may look completely unpredicted, henceforth a case of model uncertainty. Yet adding a simple rule of monetary aggregate oversight may add a proper safeguard and change that uncertainty into risk, something more measurable and possible to manage, therefore creating a tool to spot higher inflation way before it happens.

Literature

Adrian, T., and Shin, H.S. 2010. Liquidity and leverage. Journal of Financial Intermediation, Vol. 19, pp. 418–437.

Allais, M. 1987. The Credit Mechanism and Its Implications. In: G.R. Feiwel (ed.) Arrow and the Foundation of the Theory of Economic Policy. New York: New York University Press.

Alvarez, F., Lucas, R.E. Jr., and Weber, W. 2001. Interest rates and inflation. American Economic Review, Vol. 91, No. 2, pp. 219–225.

Bank of England. 2014. Money creation in the modern economy. Quarterly Bulletin, 2014 Q1.

Baumol, W.J. 1952. The transactions demand for cash: An inventory theoretic approach. Quarterly Journal of Economics, Vol. 66, No. 4, pp. 545–556.

Beck, G.W., and Wieland, V. 2007. Money in monetary policy design: A formal characterization of ECB-style cross-checking. Journal of the European Economic Association, Vol. 5, No. 2/3, Proceedings of the Twenty-First Annual Congress of the European Economic Association.

Bernanke, B.S., and Gertler, M. 1995. Inside the black box: The credit channel of monetary policy transmission. Journal of Economic Perspectives, Vol. 9, No. 4, pp. 27–48.

Bernanke, B.S., and Reinhart, V. 2004. Conducting monetary policy at very low short-term interest rates. American Economic Review, Vol. 94, No. 2, pp. 85–90.

Bernanke, B.S. 2002. Deflation: Making Sure 'It' Doesn't Happen Here. Washington D.C., Remarks before the National Economists' Club. November 21. http://www.federalreserve.gov/boarddocs/speeches/2002/20021121/default.htm

Boivin, J., Kiley M.T., and Mishkin, F.S. 2010. How Has the Monetary Transmission Mechanism Evolved Over Time? Finance and Economics Discussion Series, Federal Reserve, available at (09–30–2016): https://www.federalreserve.gov/pubs/feds/2010/201026/201026pap.pdf.

Bonam, D., and Smădu, A. 2021. The long-run effects of pandemics on inflation: Will this time be different? Economics Letters, Vol. 208, 10.1016/j.econlet.2021.110065.

Bordo, M.D. 1989. Equation of Exchange. In Money (pp. 151–156). Palgrave Macmillan UK. 10.1007/978-1-349-19804-7_17

Borio, C., and Zhu, H. 2012. Capital regulation, risk-taking and monetary policy: A missing link in the transmission mechanism? Journal of Financial Stability, Vol. 8, No. 4, pp. 236–251.

Borio, C., Hofmann, B., and Zakrajšek, E. 2023a. Does Money Growth Help Explain the Recent Inflation Surge? BIS Bulletin no. 67, January. https://www.bis.org/publ/bisbull67.pdf

Borio, C., Lombardi, M., Hofmann, B., and Zakrajšek, E. 2023b. The Two-Regime View of Inflation. BIS Papers no. 133, January. https://www.bis.org/publ/bppdf/bispap133.pdf

Brinkmeyer, H. 2015. Drivers of Bank Lending. Schriften zum europäischen Management. Springer Fachmedien Wiesbaden.

Brunner, K., and Meltzer, A. 1988. Money and credit in the monetary transmission process. American Economic Review, Vol. 78, No. 2, pp. 446–451.

Bruno, V., and Shin, H.S. 2013. Capital Flows and the Risk-Taking Channel of Monetary Policy. NBER Working Paper 18942, available at (04–10–2016): http://www.nber.org/papers/w18942.pdf

Brzoza-Brzezina, M., Kolasa, M., and Makarski, K. 2021. Monetary Policy and COVID-19. IMF Working Paper No. 2021/274, Available at SSRN: https://ssrn.com/abstract=4026503

Bundesbank. 2017. The Role of Banks, Non-banks and the Central Bank in the Money Creation Process. Monthly Report.

Burdekin, R. 2020. The US money explosion of 2020, monetarism and inflation: Plagued by history? Modern Economy, Vol. 11, pp. 1887–1900. 10.4236/me.2020.1111126.

Cagan, P. 1956. The Monetary Dynamics of Hyperinflation. In: M. Friedman (ed.) Studies in the Quantity Theory of Money, University of Chicago Press, pp. 25–117.

Cairnes, J.E. 1873. Essays in Political Economy Theoretical and Applied. London: Macmillan and Co.

Cantillon, R. 1959. Essay on the Nature of Trade in General, 1755. London: Frank Cass and Co.

Caraiani, P. 2016. The role of money in DSGE models: A forecasting perspective. Journal of Macroeconomics. Vol. 47, pp. 315–330. 10.1016/j.jmacro.2015.10.001

Claeys, G. 2014. The (Not So) Unconventional Monetary Policy of the European Central Bank Since 2008 Draft. YPFS Documents. 1936. https://elischolar.library.yale.edu/ypfs-documents/1936

De Grauwe, P., and Polan, M. 2005. Is inflation always and everywhere a monetary phenomenon? Scandinavian Journal of Economics, Vol. 107, No. 2, pp. 239–259.

Dewald, W.G., and Haug, A.A. 2004. Longer-term effects of monetary growth on real and nominal variables, major industrial countries, 1880–2001. Working Paper Series 382, European Central Bank.

Diamond, D.W., and Rajan, R.G. 2001. Liquidity risk, liquidity creation, and financial fragility: A theory of banking. Journal of Political Economy. Vol. 109, No. 2, pp. 287–327. 10.1086/319552.

Disyatat, P. 2010. The bank lending channel revisited. BIS Working Paper 297.

Dwyer, G.P. Jr., and Hafer, R.W. 1988. Is money irrelevant? Federal Reserve Bank of St. Louis Review, Vol. 70, pp. 3–17.

Dwyer, G.P. Jr., and Hafer, R.W. 1999. Are money growth and inflation still related? Federal Reserve Bank of Atlanta Economic Review, Vol. 84, pp. 32–43.

Eichenbaum, M.S., Rebelo, S., and Trabandt, M. 2021. The macroeconomics of epidemics. The Review of Financial Studies, Vol. 34, No. 11, pp. 5149–5187, November 2021. 10.1093/rfs/hhab040

English, B., Forbes, K., and Ubide, A. 2021. Monetary policy and central banking in the Covid era: Key insights and challenges for the future. In: ibidem. Monetary policy and central banking in the Covid era. Centre for Economic Policy Research.

Estrella, A. and Mishkin, F.S. 1997. Is There a Role for Monetary Aggregates

Friedman, M. 1956. The Quantity Theory of Money – A Restatement. In: M. Friedman (ed.). Studies in the Quantity Theory of Money, pp. 3–21, Chicago, IL: University of Chicago Press.

Fedak, K.M., Bernal, A., Capshaw, Z.A., and Gross, S. 2015. Applying the Bradford Hill criteria in the 21st century: How data integration has changed causal inference in molecular epidemiology. Emerging Themes of Epidemiology. Sep 30;12:14. doi: 10.1186/s12982-015-0037-4.

Fisher, I. 1933. The debt-deflation theory of Great Depressions. Econometrica, Vol. 1, pp. 337–357.

Fisher, I. 1936. 100% Money and Public Debt. (in:) Economic Forum, April–June.

Friedman, M., and Schwartz, A.J. 1963. A Monetary History of the United States, 1867–1960. Princeton, NJ: Princeton University Press.

Friedman, M. (ed.). 1969a. The Optimum Quantity of Money and Other Essays. Chicago: Aldine Publishing Company.

Friedman, M. 1956. The Quantity Theory of Money: A Restatement. (in:) Friedman 1969a.

Friedman, M. 1960. A Program for Monetary Stability. New York: Fordham University Press.

Friedman, M. 1968. The Role of Monetary Policy. (in:) M. Friedman. 1969.

Friedman, M. 1969. The Optimum Quantity of Money. In: M. Friedman (ed.). 1969a The Optimum Quantity of Money and Other Essays. Chicago: Aldine Publishing Company.

Gertler, M. and Kiyotaki, N. 2010. Financial Intermediation and Credit Policy in Business Cycle Analysis. In: Friedman, B. and Woodford, M. (eds.), Handbook of Monetary Economics, Volume 3A, North Holland: Elsevier.

Gertler, P., and Hofmann, B. 2018. Monetary facts revisited. Journal of International Money and Finance, Vol. 86, No. C, pp. 154–170.

Goodfriend, M. and King, R.G. 1997. The New Neo-classical Synthesis and the Role of Monetary Policy. In B. Bernanke and J.J. Rotemberg (eds.), NBER Macroeconomics Annual 1997, MIT Press.

Goodhart, C.A.E. 1989. The conduct of monetary policy. Economic Journal, Vol. 99, pp. 293–346.

Greenwood, J., and Hanke, S.H. 2021. On monetary growth and inflation in leading economies, 2021–2022: Relative prices and the overall price level. Journal of Applied Corporate Finance, Vol. 33, pp. 39–51. 10.1111/jacf.12479.

Gros, D., and Capolongo, A. 2019. In depth Analysis. Requested by the ECON committee, Monetary Dialogue Papers, December 2019. The Two-pillar Strategy of the ECB: Ready for a Review The Two-pillar Strategy of the ECB: Policy Department for Economic, Scientific and Quality of Life Policies Directorate-General for Internal Policies.

Hafer, R.W., and Wheelock, D.C. 2001. The Rise and Fall of a Policy Rule: Monetarism at the St. Louis Fed, 1968–86. Federal Reserve Bank of St. Louis Review, January/February 2001, pp. 1–24.

Haldane, A.G., Roberts-Sklar, M., Wieladek, T., and Young, C. 2016. QE – The story so far. Bank of England staff working paper no. 624.

Hanke, S.H., and Krus, H. 2012. World Hyperinflations. Cato Working Paper no. 8, August 15.

Heffernan, S. 1996. Modern Banking in Theory and Practice. Chichester: John Wiley and Sons.

Hellwig, M.F. 2000. Financial intermediation with risk aversion. Review of Economic Studies, Vol. 67, No. 4, pp. 719–742.

Hendrickson, J. 2023. Is the Quantity Theory Dead? Lessons from the Pandemic. Mercatus Special Study, Mercatus Center at George Mason University, Arlington, VA, January 2023.

Hume, D. 1777. Of Money, In: Essays, Moral, Political, and Literary, Liberty Fund Edition. Liberty Fund: Indianapolis.

Jabłecki, J., and Machaj, M. 2009. The regulated meltdown of 2008. Critical review. A Journal of Politics and Society. Vol. 21, No. 2–3, pp. 301–328.

Jakab, Z., and Kumhof, M. 2015. Banks are not intermediaries of loanable funds - and why this matters. Bank of England, Working Paper No. 529. https://www.bankofengland.co.uk/working-paper/2015/banks-are-not-intermediaries-of-loanable-funds-and-why-this-matters

Jeenas, P., and Lagos, R. 2022. Q-Monetary Transmission. National Bureau of Economic Research Working Paper Series, http://www.nber.org/papers/w30023.

Jiménez, G., Ongena, S., Peydró J.S., and Saurina, J. 2014. Hazardous times for monetary policy: What do twenty-three million bank loans say about the effects of monetary policy on credit risk-taking? Econometrica, Vol. 82, No. 2, pp. 463–505.

Joyce, M.A.S., Lasaosa, A., Stevens, I., and Tong, M. 2011. The financial market impact of quantitative easing in the United Kingdom. International Journal of Central Banking, Vol. 7, No. 3, pp. 113–161.

Kantor, B. 2022. Recent monetary history: A monetarist perspective. Journal of Applied Corporate Finance, Vol. 34, No. 2. 10.1111/jacf.12508

Kashyap, A., Rajan, E., and Stein, J. 2002. Banks as liquidity providers: An explanation for the coexistence of lending and deposit-taking. Journal of Finance, Vol. 57, pp. 33–73.

King, M.A. 2002. No Money, No Inflation – The Role of Money in the Economy. Bank of England Quarterly Bulletin, Summer 2002, pp. 162–177.

Koo, R.C. 2001. The Japanese economy in balance sheet recession: The real culprit is fallacy of composition, not complacency. Business Economics, Vol. 36, No. 2, pp. 15–23.

Koo, R.C. 2010. Lessons from Japan: Fighting a Balance Sheet Recession. Lecture at CFA Institute Annual Conference; available at (09–10–2016): http://www.cfapubs.org/doi/pdf/10.2469/cp.v27.n4.4

Koo, R.C. 2012. Balance Sheet Recession as the Other-Half of Macroeconomics. Nomura Research Institute; available at (09–10–2016): http://www.boeckler.de/pdf/v_2012_10_25_koo.pdf

Koo, R.C. 2014. Balance Sheet Recession Is the Reason for Secular Stagnation. In: C. Teulings and R. Baldwin (ed.). 2014. Secular Stagnation: Facts, Causes, and Cures. London: Center for Economic Policy Research.

Laidler, D. 2002. Monetary policy without money: Hamlet without the ghost. In: R. Leeson (ed.), Macroeconomics, monetary policy and financial stability: Essays in honour of Charles Freedman, Bank of Canada, pp. 111–134.

Lapavitsas, C. 2022. The return of inflation and the weakness of the side of production. The Japanese Political Economy, Vol. 48, No. 2–4, pp. 149–169, DOI:10.1080/2329194X.2022.2142613

Lepetit, A., and Fuentes-Albero, C. 2022. The limited power of monetary policy in a pandemic. European Economic Review, Elsevier, Vol. 147, No. C, pp. 1–25.

Liping, H. 2017. Hyperinflation: A World History (1st ed.). Routledge. 10.4324/9780203712061.

Locke, J. 1963. The Works of John Locke. Vol. 5. London, 1823; reprint, Aden (Germany).

London, S. 2003. Lunch with the FT: Milton Friedman. Financial Times, June 7.

Lown, C.S., and Morgan, D.P. 2002. Credit Effects in the Monetary Mechanism. FRBNY Economic Policy Review, May.

Lucas Jr., R.E. 1996. Nobel lecture: Monetary neutrality. Journal of Political Economy, Vol. 104, No. 4, pp. 661–682.

Manoj, P., and Goodhart, C.A.E. 2021. Friedman vs Phillips: A Historic Divide. VoxEU. https://cepr.org/voxeu/columns/friedman-vs-phillips-historic-divide

Masuch, K., Nicoletti-Altimari, S., Rostagno, M., and Pill, H. 2004. The role of money in monetary policymaking. BIS papers no. 19, pp. 158–191.

McCallum, B. 2001. Monetary Policy Analysis in Models Without Money. 10.3386/w8174

McCandless, G., and Weber, W. 1995. Some monetary facts. Federal Reserve Bank of Minneapolis Quarterly Reviews. Vol. 19, No. 3, pp. 2–11.

Meltzer, A.H. 1995. Monetary, credit and (other) transmission processes: A monetarist perspective. The Journal of Economic Perspectives. Vol. 9, No. 4, pp. 49–72. http://www.jstor.org/stable/2138390.

Merton, R.C., and Bodie, Z. 1993. Deposit Insurance Reform: A Functional Approach. Carnegie Rochester Conference Series on Public Policy 38.

Meyer, L.H. 2001. Does money matter? The 2001 Homer Jones Memorial Lecture, Washington University, St. Louis, Missouri, March 28, 2001, in The Federal Reserve Bank of Saint Louis Review, September/October.

Miller, M.H., and Orr, D. 1966. A model of the demand for money by firms. Quarterly Journal of Economics, Vol. 80, No. 3, pp. 413–435.

Miron, J.A., Romer, C.D., and Weil, D.N. 1993. Historical Perspectives on the Monetary Transmission Mechanism. NBER Working Paper No. 4326.

Nelson, E. 2008. Why money growth determines inflation in the long run: Answering the woodford critique. Journal of Money, Credit and Banking, Vol. 40, No. 8, pp. 1791–1814. http://www.jstor.org/stable/25483471

Pinter, J. 2022. Monetarist arithmetic at COVID-19 time: A take on how not to misapply the quantity theory of money. Economic Notes, Vol. 51, p. e12200. 10.1111/ecno.12200.

Rajan, R.G. 2006. Has finance made the world riskier? European Financial Management, Vol. 12, No. 4, pp. 499–533.

Salerno, J.T. 2006. A simple model of the theory of money prices. Quarterly Journal of Austrian Economics, Vol. 9, pp. 39–55. 10.1007/s12113-006-1023-z

Sargent, T., and Surico, P. 2011. Two illustrations of the quantity theory of money: Breakdowns and revivals. American Economic Review, Vol. 101, No. 1, pp. 109–128.

Sieroń, A. 2015. Disaggregating the credit expansion: The role of changes in banks' asset structure in the business cycle. Quarterly Journal of Austrian Economics, Vol. 18, No. 3, pp. 247–271.

Sieroń, A. 2017. The role of shadow banking in the business cycle. Quarterly Journal of Austrian Economics, Vol. 19, No. 4, pp. 309–329.

Stein, J.C. 2014. Banks as patient debt investors. American Economic Association/American Finance Association Joint Luncheon, Philadelphia, Pennsylvania, 3 January 2014.

Sumner, S. 2021. Chapter 4. The Quantity Theory of Money and the Great Inflation. The Money Illusion: Market Monetarism, the Great Recession, and the Future of Monetary Policy, Chicago: University of Chicago Press, pp. 51–63. 10.7208/chicago/9780226773711-006

Teles, P., and Zhou, R. 2005. A stable money demand: Looking for the right monetary aggregate. Federal Reserve Bank of Chicago Economic Perspectives, 1Q/2005, pp. 50–63.

Teles, P., Uhlig, H., and Valle e Azevedo, J. 2016. Is quantity theory still alive? The Economic Journal, Vol. 126, No. 591, pp. 442–464. 10.1111/ecoj.12336

Tobin, J. 1956. The interest elasticity of the transactions demand for cash. Review of Economics and Statistics, Vol. 38, No. 3, pp. 241–247.

Tobin, J. 1969. A general equilibrium approach to monetary theory. Journal of Money, Credit and Banking, Vol. 1, No. 1, pp. 15–29.

Tobin, J. 1985. Financial innovation and deregulation in perspective. Bank of Japan Monetary and Economic Studies, Vol. 3, pp. 19–29.

Van den Heuvel, S.J. 2002. Does Bank Capital Matter for Monetary Transition? FRBNY Economic Policy Review, May.

Vogel, R.C. 1974. The dynamics of inflation in Latin America, 1950–1969. American Economic Review, Vol. 64, pp. 102–114.

Walsh, C.E. 2003. Monetary Theory and Policy, 2nd ed. Cambridge, MA: MIT Press.

Werner, R. 2014. Can banks individually create money out of nothing? – The theories and the empirical evidence. International Review of Financial Analysis, Vol. 36, pp. 1–19.

Wicksell, K. 1962. Interest and Prices. New York: Sentry Press.

Wong, A. 2019. Refinancing and the Transmission of Monetary Policy to Consumption. Mimeo, Princeton University.

Woodford, M. 2008. How important is money in the conduct of monetary policy? Journal of Money, Credit and Banking, Vol. 40, No. 8, pp. 1561–1598.

Woodford, M. 2003. Interest and Prices: Foundations of a Theory of Monetary Policy. Princeton: Princeton University Press.

Zimmerman, G. 2003. Optimal monetary policy: A new Keynesian view. Quarterly Journal of Austrian Economics, Vol. 6, No. 4, pp. 61–72.

Index

Active monetary policy: after 2008 34–45; during 2020 pandemic 46–51

balance sheet channel 28, 29
Bank of England 42
Basel regulations 28
Baumol, W.J. 17, 19
Bernanke, B.S. 34, 35, 36, 37, 39, 43
BIS report 1–6
Borio, C. 1
Bouey, G. 53
Bradford Hill criteria 21, 23, 24
Bundesbank 1, 25, 42
Burdekin, R. 50

Cantillon, R. 12
capital channel of banks 28
Caraiani, P. 33
causality 14, 21
central bank 2, 4, 10, 17, 18, 25–26, 28, 30, 31–37, 39, 41–43, 45, 47, 50–54
Commercial banks 28, 30, 33, 35, 36, 37, 39, 41, 42
consumption channel 27, 28
conventional monetary policy 25–33
credit expansion, regulation on 28

De Grauwe, P. 15, 16, 20
Dewald, W.G. 13
direct inflation targeting (DIT) strategy 13, 17, 18, 19, 20, 25, 45, 46
discretionary policy 9
DIT strategy see direct inflation targeting strategy
dollar economy 36

double-digit inflation 16, 19, 20, 23, 37, 43
DSGE models 33

English, B. 47
epidemic situation, monetary policy during 47
equation of exchange 7–8, 10, 12, 16, 17, 19, 32
Estrella, A. 11
exchange rate 27

Federal Reserve 35, 37
fiscal policy 21, 28, 36
Fisher effect 26
Fisher, I. 8, 15, 17
Friedman, M. 4, 7–12, 34, 42, 43, 44

Great Depression 6, 34
Great Financial Recession 29, 34, 37, 44, 47
Greenwood, J. 50

Hafer, R.W. 10
Hanke, S.H. 22, 50
Haug, A.A. 13
Hendrickson, J. 50
Higher inflation 1, 2, 4, 45, 50, 52, 54
Hoffmann, B. 1
hyperdeflation 8
hyperinflation 8, 21–24, 26, 37, 42

illiquid instruments 29
interest rates 25–35, 41, 45, 47, 50, 53
international channel 27, 28
International Monetary Fund 15
investment channel of transmission 27
IS-LM models 28

Kantor, B. 50
King, M.A. 33
Koo, R.C. 39
Krugman, P. 43
Krus, H. 22

Lapavitsas, C. 51
Lowering inflation 44–45
Lucas Jr., R.E. 1, 13

McCandless, G. 13, 14, 15, 17
Meyer, L.H. 53
Miller, M.H. 17
Mishkin, F.S. 11
modern monetary policy 30, 32, 34
monetarism 10, 32
monetary transmission mechanism 26,
    28, 29, 30, 32, 33, 34, 36, 46
multiplier (money) theory 37

Nelson, E. 32
Neo-Wicksellian framework 31, 32
New Keynesian models 26, 31–32

on-demand deposits 37
open market operations 30, 32, 33,
    35, 37
operation twist 35
optimal monetary rule 33
Orr, D. 17
"out of thin air" (money creation) 41,
    42–43, 51

pandemic effect on inflation levels 46–51
Pinter, J. 50
Polan, M. 15, 16, 20
post-pandemic inflation 50, 51

Powell, J. 51
price movements 15
price-forming analysis 46–47

"qualitative" easing 36
quantity theory of money 4, 7, 12,
    13–20, 37, 42–43, 44, 46, 52

risk channel 28, 29, 30

Sargent, T. 16
Schwartz, A. 8, 9
Smith, A. 12
St. Louis models 11
Surico, P. 16

Taylor rule 31
Teles, P. 16, 17, 18, 19
Tobin, J. 17, 19, 27

unconventional monetary policy 34–45

Walrasian equilibrium framework 26
Walsh, C.E. 14, 15
Weber, W. 13, 14, 15, 17
Weimar Republic 36, 37
Werner, R. 42, 51
Wheelock, D.C. 10
Wicksell, K. 31
Woodford, M. 30, 31, 32, 34

X-type economies 15–17, 19, 20

Y-type economies 15, 21

Zakrajšek, E. 1
Zhou, R. 16, 17, 18, 19